NEW OFF.

Online Study Secrets Course!

Dear Customer,

Struggle with tests? Short on time? Not sure where to even *start* studying? Mometrix has designed a new Study Secrets Course to help every student, no matter what study scenario you are in.

This online course guides you through the full process, from study preparation to test day, so you'll be ready to ace your next exam. The Study Secrets Course contains **14 in-depth lessons** that break down top study strategies, **15+ video reviews** that walk you step by step through each topic, and **5 downloadable resources** to help you apply the strategies.

Online Study Secrets Course

Course Features:

- Techniques to Conquer Procrastination
- Steps to Building a Study Plan
- 7 Effective Note-Taking Methods
- Test-Taking Tips
- Memory Techniques and Mnemonics
- 50 Quick and Unusual Study Tips
- How to Create SMART Goals
- How to Study Math
- And much more!

Everyone learns differently, so we've tailored our Study Secrets Course to ensure that every learner has what they need to prepare for their upcoming exam or semester.

To purchase this course and start studying, visit us at mometrix.com/university/studysecrets or simply scan this QR code with your smartphone.

If you have any questions or concerns, please contact us at support@mometrix.com.

ACCESS YOUR ONLINE RESOURCES

DON'T MISS OUT ON THE ONLINE RESOURCES INCLUDED WITH YOUR PURCHASE!

Your purchase of this product unlocks access to our Online Resources page. Elevate your study experience with our **interactive practice test interface**, along with all of the additional resources that we couldn't include in this book.

Flip to the Online Resources section at the end of this book to find the link and a QR code to get started!

FCLE
Exam Prep Book

2 Full-Length Practice Tests

Florida Civic Literacy Secrets Study Guide

Includes Detailed Answer Explanations

Written and edited by Matthew Bowling

Printed in the United States of America

This paper meets the requirements of ANSI/NISO Z39.48-1992 (Permanence of Paper).

Mometrix offers volume discount pricing to institutions. For more information or a price quote, please contact our sales department at sales@mometrix.com or 888-248-1219.

ISBN 13: 978-1-5167-2814-5
ISBN 10: 1-5167-2814-9

DEAR FUTURE EXAM SUCCESS STORY

First of all, **THANK YOU** for purchasing Mometrix study materials!

Second, congratulations! You are one of the few determined test-takers who are committed to doing whatever it takes to excel on your exam. **You have come to the right place.** We developed these study materials with one goal in mind: to deliver you the information you need in a format that's concise and easy to use.

In addition to optimizing your guide for the content of the test, we've outlined our recommended steps for breaking down the preparation process into small, attainable goals so you can make sure you stay on track.

We've also analyzed the entire test-taking process, identifying the most common pitfalls and showing how you can overcome them and be ready for any curveball the test throws you.

Standardized testing is one of the biggest obstacles on your road to success, which only increases the importance of doing well in the high-pressure, high-stakes environment of test day. Your results on this test could have a significant impact on your future, and this guide provides the information and practical advice to help you achieve your full potential on test day.

Your success is our success

We would love to hear from you! If you would like to share the story of your exam success or if you have any questions or comments in regard to our products, please contact us at **800-673-8175** or **support@mometrix.com**.

Thanks again for your business and we wish you continued success!

Sincerely,
The Mometrix Test Preparation Team

TABLE OF CONTENTS

Introduction

Thank you for purchasing this resource! You have made the choice to prepare yourself for a test that could have a huge impact on your future, and this guide is designed to help you be fully ready for test day. Obviously, it's important to have a solid understanding of the test material, but you also need to be prepared for the unique environment and stressors of the test, so that you can perform to the best of your abilities.

For this purpose, the first section that appears in this guide is the **Secret Keys**. We've devoted countless hours to meticulously researching what works and what doesn't, and we've boiled down our findings to the five most impactful steps you can take to improve your performance on the test. We start at the beginning with study planning and move through the preparation process, all the way to the testing strategies that will help you get the most out of what you know when you're finally sitting in front of the test.

We recommend that you start preparing for your test as far in advance as possible. However, if you've bought this guide as a last-minute study resource and only have a few days before your test, we recommend that you skip over the first two Secret Keys since they address a long-term study plan.

If you struggle with **test anxiety**, we strongly encourage you to check out our recommendations for how you can overcome it. Test anxiety is a formidable foe, but it can be beaten, and we want to make sure you have the tools you need to defeat it.

1

Secret Key #1 – Plan Big, Study Small

There's a lot riding on your performance. If you want to ace this test, you're going to need to keep your skills sharp and the material fresh in your mind. You need a plan that lets you review everything you need to know while still fitting in your schedule. We'll break this strategy down into three categories.

Information Organization

Start with the information you already have: the official test outline. From this, you can make a complete list of all the concepts you need to cover before the test. Organize these concepts into groups that can be studied together, and create a list of any related vocabulary you need to learn so you can brush up on any difficult terms. You'll want to keep this vocabulary list handy once you actually start studying since you may need to add to it along the way.

Time Management

Once you have your set of study concepts, decide how to spread them out over the time you have left before the test. Break your study plan into small, clear goals so you have a manageable task for each day and know exactly what you're doing. Then just focus on one small step at a time. When you manage your time this way, you don't need to spend hours at a time studying. Studying a small block of content for a short period each day helps you retain information better and avoid stressing over how much you have left to do. You can relax knowing that you have a plan to cover everything in time. In order for this strategy to be effective though, you have to start studying early and stick to your schedule. Avoid the exhaustion and futility that comes from last-minute cramming!

Study Environment

The environment you study in has a big impact on your learning. Studying in a coffee shop, while probably more enjoyable, is not likely to be as fruitful as studying in a quiet room. It's important to keep distractions to a minimum. You're only planning to study for a short block of time, so make the most of it. Don't pause to check your phone or get up to find a snack. It's also important to **avoid multitasking**. Research has consistently shown that multitasking will make your studying dramatically less effective. Your study area should also be comfortable and well-lit so you don't have the distraction of straining your eyes or sitting on an uncomfortable chair.

 The time of day you study is also important. You want to be rested and alert. Don't wait until just before bedtime. Study when you'll be most likely to comprehend and remember. Even better, if you know what time of day your test will be, set that time aside for study. That way your brain will be used to working on that subject at that specific time and you'll have a better chance of recalling information.

Finally, it can be helpful to team up with others who are studying for the same test. Your actual studying should be done in as isolated an environment as possible, but the work of organizing the information and setting up the study plan can be divided up. In between study sessions, you can discuss with your teammates the concepts that you're all studying and quiz each other on the details. Just be sure that your teammates are as serious about the test as you are. If you find that your study time is being replaced with social time, you might need to find a new team.

Secret Key #2 – Make Your Studying Count

You're devoting a lot of time and effort to preparing for this test, so you want to be absolutely certain it will pay off. This means doing more than just reading the content and hoping you can remember it on test day. It's important to make every minute of study count. There are two main areas you can focus on to make your studying count.

Retention

It doesn't matter how much time you study if you can't remember the material. You need to make sure you are retaining the concepts. To check your retention of the information you're learning, try recalling it at later times with minimal prompting. Try carrying around flashcards and glance at one or two from time to time or ask a friend who's also studying for the test to quiz you.

To enhance your retention, look for ways to put the information into practice so that you can apply it rather than simply recalling it. If you're using the information in practical ways, it will be much easier to remember. Similarly, it helps to solidify a concept in your mind if you're not only reading it to yourself but also explaining it to someone else. Ask a friend to let you teach them about a concept you're a little shaky on (or speak aloud to an imaginary audience if necessary). As you try to summarize, define, give examples, and answer your friend's questions, you'll understand the concepts better and they will stay with you longer. Finally, step back for a big picture view and ask yourself how each piece of information fits with the whole subject. When you link the different concepts together and see them working together as a whole, it's easier to remember the individual components.

Finally, practice showing your work on any multi-step problems, even if you're just studying. Writing out each step you take to solve a problem will help solidify the process in your mind, and you'll be more likely to remember it during the test.

Modality

Modality simply refers to the means or method by which you study. Choosing a study modality that fits your own individual learning style is crucial. No two people learn best in exactly the same way, so it's important to know your strengths and use them to your advantage.

For example, if you learn best by visualization, focus on visualizing a concept in your mind and draw an image or a diagram. Try color-coding your notes, illustrating them, or creating symbols that will trigger your mind to recall a learned concept. If you learn best by hearing or discussing information, find a study partner who learns the same way or read aloud to yourself. Think about how to put the information in your own words. Imagine that you are giving a lecture on the topic and record yourself so you can listen to it later.

For any learning style, flashcards can be helpful. Organize the information so you can take advantage of spare moments to review. Underline key words or phrases. Use different colors for different categories. Mnemonic devices (such as creating a short list in which every item starts with the same letter) can also help with retention. Find what works best for you and use it to store the information in your mind most effectively and easily.

Secret Key #3 – Practice the Right Way

Your success on test day depends not only on how many hours you put into preparing, but also on whether you prepared the right way. It's good to check along the way to see if your studying is paying off. One of the most effective ways to do this is by taking practice tests to evaluate your progress. Practice tests are useful because they show exactly where you need to improve. Every time you take a practice test, pay special attention to these three groups of questions:

- The questions you got wrong
- The questions you had to guess on, even if you guessed right
- The questions you found difficult or slow to work through

This will show you exactly what your weak areas are, and where you need to devote more study time. Ask yourself why each of these questions gave you trouble. Was it because you didn't understand the material? Was it because you didn't remember the vocabulary? Do you need more repetitions on this type of question to build speed and confidence? Dig into those questions and figure out how you can strengthen your weak areas as you go back to review the material.

 Additionally, many practice tests have a section explaining the answer choices. It can be tempting to read the explanation and think that you now have a good understanding of the concept. However, an explanation likely only covers part of the question's broader context. Even if the explanation makes perfect sense, **go back and investigate** every concept related to the question until you're positive you have a thorough understanding.

As you go along, keep in mind that the practice test is just that: practice. Memorizing these questions and answers will not be very helpful on the actual test because it is unlikely to have any of the same exact questions. If you only know the right answers to the sample questions, you won't be prepared for the real thing. **Study the concepts** until you understand them fully, and then you'll be able to answer any question that shows up on the test.

It's important to wait on the practice tests until you're ready. If you take a test on your first day of study, you may be overwhelmed by the amount of material covered and how much you need to learn. Work up to it gradually.

On test day, you'll need to be prepared for answering questions, managing your time, and using the test-taking strategies you've learned. It's a lot to balance, like a mental marathon that will have a big impact on your future. Like training for a marathon, you'll need to start slowly and work your way up. When test day arrives, you'll be ready.

Start with the strategies you've read in the first two Secret Keys—plan your course and study in the way that works best for you. If you have time, consider using multiple study resources to get different approaches to the same concepts. It can be helpful to see difficult concepts from more than one angle. Then find a good source for practice tests. Many times, the test website will suggest potential study resources or provide sample tests.

Practice Test Strategy

If you're able to find at least three practice tests, we recommend this strategy:

UNTIMED AND OPEN-BOOK PRACTICE

Take the first test with no time constraints and with your notes and study guide handy. Take your time and focus on applying the strategies you've learned.

TIMED AND OPEN-BOOK PRACTICE

Take the second practice test open-book as well, but set a timer and practice pacing yourself to finish in time.

TIMED AND CLOSED-BOOK PRACTICE

Take any other practice tests as if it were test day. Set a timer and put away your study materials. Sit at a table or desk in a quiet room, imagine yourself at the testing center, and answer questions as quickly and accurately as possible.

Keep repeating timed and closed-book tests on a regular basis until you run out of practice tests or it's time for the actual test. Your mind will be ready for the schedule and stress of test day, and you'll be able to focus on recalling the material you've learned.

Secret Key #4 – Pace Yourself

Once you're fully prepared for the material on the test, your biggest challenge on test day will be managing your time. Just knowing that the clock is ticking can make you panic even if you have plenty of time left. Work on pacing yourself so you can build confidence against the time constraints of the exam. Pacing is a difficult skill to master, especially in a high-pressure environment, so **practice is vital**.

Set time expectations for your pace based on how much time is available. For example, if a section has 60 questions and the time limit is 30 minutes, you know you have to average 30 seconds or less per question in order to answer them all. Although 30 seconds is the hard limit, set 25 seconds per question as your goal, so you reserve extra time to spend on harder questions. When you budget extra time for the harder questions, you no longer have any reason to stress when those questions take longer to answer.

Don't let this time expectation distract you from working through the test at a calm, steady pace, but keep it in mind so you don't spend too much time on any one question. Recognize that taking extra time on one question you don't understand may keep you from answering two that you do understand later in the test. If your time limit for a question is up and you're still not sure of the answer, mark it and move on, and come back to it later if the time and the test format allow. If the testing format doesn't allow you to return to earlier questions, just make an educated guess; then put it out of your mind and move on.

On the easier questions, be careful not to rush. It may seem wise to hurry through them so you have more time for the challenging ones, but it's not worth missing one if you know the concept and just didn't take the time to read the question fully. Work efficiently but make sure you understand the question and have looked at all of the answer choices, since more than one may seem right at first.

Even if you're paying attention to the time, you may find yourself a little behind at some point. You should speed up to get back on track, but do so wisely. Don't panic; just take a few seconds less on each question until you're caught up. Don't guess without thinking, but do look through the answer choices and eliminate any you know are wrong. If you can get down to two choices, it is often worthwhile to guess from those. Once you've chosen an answer, move on and don't dwell on any that you skipped or had to hurry through. If a question was taking too long, chances are it was one of the harder ones, so you weren't as likely to get it right anyway.

On the other hand, if you find yourself getting ahead of schedule, it may be beneficial to slow down a little. The more quickly you work, the more likely you are to make a careless mistake that will affect your score. You've budgeted time for each question, so don't be afraid to spend that time. Practice an efficient but careful pace to get the most out of the time you have.

Secret Key #5 – Have a Plan for Guessing

When you're taking the test, you may find yourself stuck on a question. Some of the answer choices seem better than others, but you don't see the one answer choice that is obviously correct. What do you do?

The scenario described above is very common, yet most test takers have not effectively prepared for it. Developing and practicing a plan for guessing may be one of the single most effective uses of your time as you get ready for the exam.

In developing your plan for guessing, there are three questions to address:

- When should you start the guessing process?
- How should you narrow down the choices?
- Which answer should you choose?

When to Start the Guessing Process

Unless your plan for guessing is to select C every time (which, despite its merits, is not what we recommend), you need to leave yourself enough time to apply your answer elimination strategies. Since you have a limited amount of time for each question, that means that if you're going to give yourself the best shot at guessing correctly, you have to decide quickly whether or not you will guess.

Of course, the best-case scenario is that you don't have to guess at all, so first, see if you can answer the question based on your knowledge of the subject and basic reasoning skills. Focus on the key words in the question and try to jog your memory of related topics. Give yourself a chance to bring the knowledge to mind, but once you realize that you don't have (or you can't access) the knowledge you need to answer the question, it's time to start the guessing process.

It's almost always better to start the guessing process too early than too late. It only takes a few seconds to remember something and answer the question from knowledge. Carefully eliminating wrong answer choices takes longer. Plus, going through the process of eliminating answer choices can actually help jog your memory.

Summary: Start the guessing process as soon as you decide that you can't answer the question based on your knowledge.

How to Narrow Down the Choices

The next chapter in this book (**Test-Taking Strategies**) includes a wide range of strategies for how to approach questions and how to look for answer choices to eliminate. You will definitely want to read those carefully, practice them, and figure out which ones work best for you. Here though, we're going to address a mindset rather than a particular strategy.

Your odds of guessing an answer correctly depend on how many options you are choosing from.

Number of options left	5	4	3	2	1
Odds of guessing correctly	20%	25%	33%	50%	100%

You can see from this chart just how valuable it is to be able to eliminate incorrect answers and make an educated guess, but there are two things that many test takers do that cause them to miss out on the benefits of guessing:

- Accidentally eliminating the correct answer
- Selecting an answer based on an impression

We'll look at the first one here, and the second one in the next section.

To avoid accidentally eliminating the correct answer, we recommend a thought exercise called **the $5 challenge**. In this challenge, you only eliminate an answer choice from contention if you are willing to bet $5 on it being wrong. Why $5? Five dollars is a small but not insignificant amount of money. It's an amount you could afford to lose but wouldn't want to throw away. And while losing

$5 once might not hurt too much, doing it twenty times will set you back $100. In the same way, each small decision you make—eliminating a choice here, guessing on a question there—won't by itself impact your score very much, but when you put them all together, they can make a big difference. By holding each answer choice elimination decision to a higher standard, you can reduce the risk of accidentally eliminating the correct answer.

The $5 challenge can also be applied in a positive sense: If you are willing to bet $5 that an answer choice *is* correct, go ahead and mark it as correct.

Summary: Only eliminate an answer choice if you are willing to bet $5 that it is wrong.

8

Which Answer to Choose

You're taking the test. You've run into a hard question and decided you'll have to guess. You've eliminated all the answer choices you're willing to bet $5 on. Now you have to pick an answer. Why do we even need to talk about this? Why can't you just pick whichever one you feel like when the time comes?

The answer to these questions is that if you don't come into the test with a plan, you'll rely on your impression to select an answer choice, and if you do that, you risk falling into a trap. The test writers know that everyone who takes their test will be guessing on some of the questions, so they intentionally write wrong answer choices to seem plausible. You still have to pick an answer though, and if the wrong answer choices are designed to look right, how can you ever be sure that you're not falling for their trap? The best solution we've found to this dilemma is to take the decision out of your hands entirely. Here is the process we recommend:

Once you've eliminated any choices that you are confident (willing to bet $5) are wrong, select the first remaining choice as your answer.

Whether you choose to select the first remaining choice, the second, or the last, the important thing is that you use some preselected standard. Using this approach guarantees that you will not be enticed into selecting an answer choice that looks right, because you are not basing your decision on how the answer choices look.

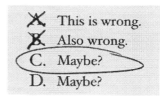

This is not meant to make you question your knowledge. Instead, it is to help you recognize the difference between your knowledge and your impressions. There's a huge difference between thinking an answer is right because of what you know, and thinking an answer is right because it looks or sounds like it should be right.

Summary: To ensure that your selection is appropriately random, make a predetermined selection from among all answer choices you have not eliminated.

Test-Taking Strategies

This section contains a list of test-taking strategies that you may find helpful as you work through the test. By taking what you know and applying logical thought, you can maximize your chances of answering any question correctly!

It is very important to realize that every question is different and every person is different: no single strategy will work on every question, and no single strategy will work for every person. That's why we've included all of them here, so you can try them out and determine which ones work best for different types of questions and which ones work best for you.

Question Strategies

⊘ READ CAREFULLY

Read the question and the answer choices carefully. Don't miss the question because you misread the terms. You have plenty of time to read each question thoroughly and make sure you understand what is being asked. Yet a happy medium must be attained, so don't waste too much time. You must read carefully and efficiently.

⊘ CONTEXTUAL CLUES

Look for contextual clues. If the question includes a word you are not familiar with, look at the immediate context for some indication of what the word might mean. Contextual clues can often give you all the information you need to decipher the meaning of an unfamiliar word. Even if you can't determine the meaning, you may be able to narrow down the possibilities enough to make a solid guess at the answer to the question.

⊘ PREFIXES

If you're having trouble with a word in the question or answer choices, try dissecting it. Take advantage of every clue that the word might include. Prefixes can be a huge help. Usually, they allow you to determine a basic meaning. *Pre-* means before, *post-* means after, *pro-* is positive, *de-* is negative. From prefixes, you can get an idea of the general meaning of the word and try to put it into context.

⊘ HEDGE WORDS

Watch out for critical hedge words, such as *likely, may, can, sometimes, often, almost, mostly, usually, generally, rarely,* and *sometimes.* Question writers insert these hedge phrases to cover every possibility. Often an answer choice will be wrong simply because it leaves no room for exception. Be on guard for answer choices that have definitive words such as *exactly* and *always.*

⊘ SWITCHBACK WORDS

Stay alert for *switchbacks.* These are the words and phrases frequently used to alert you to shifts in thought. The most common switchback words are *but, although,* and *however.* Others include *nevertheless, on the other hand, even though, while, in spite of, despite,* and *regardless of.* Switchback words are important to catch because they can change the direction of the question or an answer choice.

10

⊘ FACE VALUE

When in doubt, use common sense. Accept the situation in the problem at face value. Don't read too much into it. These problems will not require you to make wild assumptions. If you have to go beyond creativity and warp time or space in order to have an answer choice fit the question, then you should move on and consider the other answer choices. These are normal problems rooted in reality. The applicable relationship or explanation may not be readily apparent, but it is there for you to figure out. Use your common sense to interpret anything that isn't clear.

Answer Choice Strategies

⊘ ANSWER SELECTION

The most thorough way to pick an answer choice is to identify and eliminate wrong answers until only one is left, then confirm it is the correct answer. Sometimes an answer choice may immediately seem right, but be careful. The test writers will usually put more than one reasonable answer choice on each question, so take a second to read all of them and make sure that the other choices are not equally obvious. As long as you have time left, it is better to read every answer choice than to pick the first one that looks right without checking the others.

⊘ ANSWER CHOICE FAMILIES

An answer choice family consists of two (in rare cases, three) answer choices that are very similar in construction and cannot all be true at the same time. If you see two answer choices that are direct opposites or parallels, one of them is usually the correct answer. For instance, if one answer choice says that quantity x increases and another either says that quantity x decreases (opposite) or says that quantity y increases (parallel), then those answer choices would fall into the same family. An answer choice that doesn't match the construction of the answer choice family is more likely to be incorrect. Most questions will not have answer choice families, but when they do appear, you should be prepared to recognize them.

⊘ ELIMINATE ANSWERS

Eliminate answer choices as soon as you realize they are wrong, but make sure you consider all possibilities. If you are eliminating answer choices and realize that the last one you are left with is also wrong, don't panic. Start over and consider each choice again. There may be something you missed the first time that you will realize on the second pass.

⊘ AVOID FACT TRAPS

Don't be distracted by an answer choice that is factually true but doesn't answer the question. You are looking for the choice that answers the question. Stay focused on what the question is asking for so you don't accidentally pick an answer that is true but incorrect. Always go back to the question and make sure the answer choice you've selected actually answers the question and is not merely a true statement.

⊘ EXTREME STATEMENTS

In general, you should avoid answers that put forth extreme actions as standard practice or proclaim controversial ideas as established fact. An answer choice that states the "process should be used in certain situations, if…" is much more likely to be correct than one that states the "process should be discontinued completely." The first is a calm rational statement and doesn't even make a definitive, uncompromising stance, using a hedge word *if* to provide wiggle room, whereas the second choice is far more extreme.

⊘ Benchmark

As you read through the answer choices and you come across one that seems to answer the question well, mentally select that answer choice. This is not your final answer, but it's the one that will help you evaluate the other answer choices. The one that you selected is your benchmark or standard for judging each of the other answer choices. Every other answer choice must be compared to your benchmark. That choice is correct until proven otherwise by another answer choice beating it. If you find a better answer, then that one becomes your new benchmark. Once you've decided that no other choice answers the question as well as your benchmark, you have your final answer.

⊘ Predict the Answer

Before you even start looking at the answer choices, it is often best to try to predict the answer. When you come up with the answer on your own, it is easier to avoid distractions and traps because you will know exactly what to look for. The right answer choice is unlikely to be word-for-word what you came up with, but it should be a close match. Even if you are confident that you have the right answer, you should still take the time to read each option before moving on.

General Strategies

⊘ Tough Questions

If you are stumped on a problem or it appears too hard or too difficult, don't waste time. Move on! Remember though, if you can quickly check for obviously incorrect answer choices, your chances of guessing correctly are greatly improved. Before you completely give up, at least try to knock out a couple of possible answers. Eliminate what you can and then guess at the remaining answer choices before moving on.

⊘ Check Your Work

Since you will probably not know every term listed and the answer to every question, it is important that you get credit for the ones that you do know. Don't miss any questions through careless mistakes. If at all possible, try to take a second to look back over your answer selection and make sure you've selected the correct answer choice and haven't made a costly careless mistake (such as marking an answer choice that you didn't mean to mark). This quick double check should more than pay for itself in caught mistakes for the time it costs.

⊘ Pace Yourself

It's easy to be overwhelmed when you're looking at a page full of questions; your mind is confused and full of random thoughts, and the clock is ticking down faster than you would like. Calm down and maintain the pace that you have set for yourself. Especially as you get down to the last few minutes of the test, don't let the small numbers on the clock make you panic. As long as you are on track by monitoring your pace, you are guaranteed to have time for each question.

⊘ Don't Rush

It is very easy to make errors when you are in a hurry. Maintaining a fast pace in answering questions is pointless if it makes you miss questions that you would have gotten right otherwise. Test writers like to include distracting information and wrong answers that seem right. Taking a little extra time to avoid careless mistakes can make all the difference in your test score. Find a pace that allows you to be confident in the answers that you select.

⊘ Keep Moving

Panicking will not help you pass the test, so do your best to stay calm and keep moving. Taking deep breaths and going through the answer elimination steps you practiced can help to break through a stress barrier and keep your pace.

Final Notes

The combination of a solid foundation of content knowledge and the confidence that comes from practicing your plan for applying that knowledge is the key to maximizing your performance on test day. As your foundation of content knowledge is built up and strengthened, you'll find that the strategies included in this chapter become more and more effective in helping you quickly sift through the distractions and traps of the test to isolate the correct answer.

Now that you're preparing to move forward into the test content chapters of this book, be sure to keep your goal in mind. As you read, think about how you will be able to apply this information on the test. If you've already seen sample questions for the test and you have an idea of the question format and style, try to come up with questions of your own that you can answer based on what you're reading. This will give you valuable practice applying your knowledge in the same ways you can expect to on test day.

Good luck and good studying!

14

Principles and Practices of American Democracy

The Social Contract

AMERICAN DEMOCRACY

American democracy can be understood as a system by which power is vested in the people. This concept, known as **popular sovereignty**, allows citizens to engage with and give legitimacy to the government through the electoral process. The democratic system in the United States of America is based on several other foundational principles, including the rule of law, a limited government, and the separation of powers. The **rule of law**—or the notion that no one who resides in a state is above the law, regardless of their position in society—supports a **limited government** in which the power of the government is limited by law. The **separation of powers** also plays a vital role in the United States government, as it ensures that power is divided between different levels and branches of the government. The philosophy behind American democracy is that these principles combine to create a system of governance that puts the constituents first and ensures the government is established by the people in a manner that prevents future abuses of power.

SOCIAL CONTRACT THEORY

Social contract theory is an Enlightenment-era (1685–1815) philosophy regarding the relationship between citizens and the legal code developed to govern society. To put it more simply, it deals with the relationship between those who rule and those who are ruled. The theory states that, in general, the actions of a person, whether political or otherwise, are guided by a hypothetical contract with the government. As part of this perceived contract, a person leaves the **state of nature**—the environment in which humans exist prior to governmental involvement where no societal structure or legal code guides human behavior—and refrains from certain actions in exchange for protection and other benefits from the government, as well as to promote the public good. The social contract is only seen as valid if it is based on the consent of the governed. In turn, the consent of the governed provides legitimacy to the government. Many Enlightenment-era theorists contributed to social contract theory, including Thomas Hobbes, John Locke, and Jean-Jacques Rousseau, among others.

CONTRIBUTIONS OF JOHN LOCKE TO SOCIAL CONTRACT THEORY

John Locke (1632–1704), a prominent Enlightenment-era philosopher, significantly contributed to **social contract theory**. Locke perceived the natural world to be one in which the law of nature encouraged individuals to respect the natural rights of life, liberty, and property. Despite these conditions, Locke believed individuals still choose to establish an impartial government that can handle disputes and assess alleged damages, ultimately leaving **the state of nature** behind. Locke theorized that in order for citizens to willingly participate in the social contract, the government must effectively protect the natural rights of citizens, such as the right to private property. Furthermore, as a result of the social contract, leaders who failed to adequately protect natural rights could and should be overthrown by the citizenry and replaced by a more suitable alternative. Locke's theory focused heavily on the **consent of the governed**, a philosophy based on the notion that a government can only be legitimate if the citizenry agrees to its governance, as well as the belief that citizens must accept the decisions of the majority of the legislature. It is important to note, however, that Locke did not believe that the legislature serves as absolute authority because the power to select the legislature rests with the citizens themselves.

15

Checks and Balances and Separation of Powers

INFLUENCE OF BARON DE MONTESQUIEU ON THE CONCEPT OF LIMITED GOVERNMENT

In his treatise *The Spirit of Law*, the Enlightenment thinker Baron de Montesquieu (1689–1755) outlined the concept of **separation of powers**. Montesquieu theorized that in order to prevent power from falling into the hands of one individual or a small group of governmental elites, a **tripartite system** should be put into place. Within this system, each branch of government must be separate and must possess the ability to exercise distinct powers. Although John Locke is credited for explaining the importance of dividing legislative and executive powers, Montesquieu expanded on the theory, highlighting the need for separate entities to hold judicial, executive, and legislative powers. For example, Montesquieu stated that if judicial powers were exercised by the legislative or executive branch instead of a separate judicial institution or branch, then true liberty would not be possible. When drafting the United States Constitution, the framers ultimately borrowed heavily from Montesquieu to develop the three separate branches of government—the executive, judicial, and legislative branches—each with its own specific powers and responsibilities. Furthermore, the introduction of checks and balances, a constitutional provision that allows each branch of government to take action against another to limit its power, was also built based on Montesquieu's theory.

INCORPORATION OF THE SEPARATION OF POWERS INTO THE US CONSTITUTION

After US colonists had witnessed and experienced the British monarchy's abuses of power, the Founding Fathers wanted to ensure that no such usurpations could occur within their new governmental system. The framers of the US Constitution believed that to prevent such abuse of power—and ultimately to limit the government's overall power—power should be divided between the executive, legislative, and judicial branches of government. The US Constitution includes **enumerated powers** for each branch that are expressly listed, as well as **implied powers** which have been interpreted to belong to specific branches over the course of US history. Article I of the US Constitution establishes the Legislative Branch and details the powers vested within that particular institution, while Articles II and III pertain to the Executive and Judicial Branches, respectively. Furthermore, the framers instituted a system of checks and balances designed to ensure that each branch of the government could "check" another branch and prevent it from becoming too powerful. For example, although the Legislative Branch has the power to enact laws, each bill must be signed into law by the President of the United States, who is the head of the Executive Branch. The framers ultimately hoped that by structuring the government using the **separation of powers**, the government's ability to overstep and exercise power tyrannically would be limited.

Rule of Law and Due Process

THE RULE OF LAW

The **rule of law** represents an essential component of any democratic government. According to this principle, all individuals, businesses, and government entities are held accountable for the same legal codes. When laws are created and enforced, they must be regulated to ensure equality and fairness for all. Overall, the rule of law centers on the concept that no one is above the law. In the United States and other democratic states, the rule of law ensures that the rights of all people are protected and helps prevent the abuse of power by government officials. For example, a government official accused of fraudulent behavior in his personal life would be adjudicated in the same fashion and subjected to the same legal protocols as an individual who works outside of the governmental sector. Ultimately, the rule of law helps to promote accountability for elected officials and to maintain an orderly society in which citizens understand that laws are applied equitably for all regardless of status or social standing.

DUE PROCESS AND THE PROMOTION OF FAIRNESS WITHIN THE JUSTICE SYSTEM

Due process ensures that the government follows specific procedures in situations where an individual's basic rights are at stake. It is used to promote fairness and equity under the law and safeguard against mistreatment by the government. Two primary types of due process exist: procedural and substantive. **Procedural due process** focuses on the fairness of the judicial process, while **substantive due process** focuses on protecting individuals from governmental interference and infringements on natural rights. The Due Process Clause of the Fifth and Fourteenth Amendments to the US Constitution guarantees the right to due process. The Fifth Amendment protects against federal due process infringements, while the Fourteenth Amendment protects against state due process infringements. Ultimately, many due process protections are provided by the US Constitution, including the right to a fair trial before a jury of peers, protection against double jeopardy, the right to confront witnesses, and protection against self-incrimination.

OPERATION OF THE JUSTICE SYSTEM IN US SOCIETY

The ultimate aim of the justice system is to maintain law and order by protecting US society and equitably enforcing laws. The **justice system** is made up of three primary components: the court system, the correctional system, and law enforcement agencies. Within the justice system, law enforcement agencies investigate reported criminal behavior, the court system analyzes and evaluates evidence and determines the innocence or guilt of those accused of criminal behavior, and the correctional system punishes and rehabilitates those found guilty. The operation of the justice system and the process by which an individual is adjudicated through the various steps of the criminal justice process are governed by the US Constitution, which seeks to ensure the fair and equitable treatment of the accused. Due process protections such as the right to confront witnesses and the right to appeal a judge's decision represent important ways the power of the justice system is limited while ensuring that all citizens are treated fairly.

17

Equality Under the Law

CONCEPT OF EQUAL PROTECTION UNDER THE LAW

The US Constitution guarantees the right to equal protection under the law. The Fourteenth Amendment was ratified in 1868 as a means of extending citizenship to recently freed slaves and to protect their civil liberties. The **Equal Protection Clause** of the Fourteenth Amendment ensures that no state denies equal protection to individuals facing similar circumstances. Although the provision initially applied only to the states, in *Bolling v Short* **(1954)**, the Supreme Court ruled that the provision also applies to the federal government through the process of reverse incorporation. Although the Supreme Court only applied the Equal Protection Clause to cases of racial discrimination initially, the Warren Court of the 1960s transformed its use, applying the doctrine to a variety of situations, including sexual discrimination and voting rights.

EQUAL TREATMENT AND PROTECTIONS UNDER THE LAW

Although all US citizens are guaranteed equal treatment under the law by virtue of the Fourteenth Amendment of the Constitution, this does not necessarily mean all will experience equal outcomes. The government must treat individuals similarly when they are encountering similar circumstances; however, it cannot and will not guarantee that all individuals will experience the same outcome. For example, all US citizens who face criminal proceedings are entitled to a trial by jury. Guaranteeing equal outcomes in such a situation would be inappropriate because, despite all being entitled to the presumption of innocence, not all those facing criminal proceedings will be innocent, and only some will be acquitted of the crimes for which they are accused. The same mentality applies to economic interactions. For example, although all US citizens should have the opportunity to apply for job positions of their choice and engage in a hiring process free of discrimination, each applicant should not receive a job offer simply because they applied. Ultimately, this provision ensures that all citizens are treated fairly while also accounting for individual decisions and actions.

Popular Sovereignty

HISTORY AND ROLE OF POPULAR SOVEREIGNTY

Popular sovereignty is an essential tenet of US governmental policy. Within a government based on popular sovereignty, power is derived from the people and can only be seen as legitimate if it effectively serves the people's will. Consequently, a government that has been established by the free will of the people must work to serve those people, as sovereignty ultimately rests in their hands. The history of popular sovereignty in the United States began with the **Declaration of Independence (1776)**, in which the authors stated that legitimate governments attain their power from the consent of the governed. This definition of governmental legitimacy was a stark contrast to the relationship between the American colonists and the British monarchy, who denied the colonists representation in the British Parliament. The notion of popular sovereignty can also be found in several places within the US Constitution, including the **Preamble**, through which the framers establish that the United States has been developed and granted legitimacy by the people themselves.

Natural Rights and Natural Law

NATURAL RIGHTS AND NATURAL LAW

The concept of **natural rights** comes from the idea that certain privileges exist to which all humans are entitled regardless of cultural practices or government policies. These rights are seen as universal and unalienable, and they include the rights to life, liberty, and property. Such rights are granted to humans by nature and cannot be impeded by government bodies without due process. **John Locke** (1632–1704), an Enlightenment-era (1685–1815) philosopher, is widely credited with developing the concept of natural rights. Many believe that the concept of natural rights evolved from **natural law**, a theory that states that all humans come into the world with a moral compass that serves as a guide for their interactions. This intrinsic sense of right versus wrong exists within most humans and is not established by governing bodies or leaders. Both natural rights and natural law represent an important basis of the United States government that can be identified in many important foundational documents, such as the Declaration of Independence (1776) and the US Constitution (1787).

INCORPORATION OF NATURAL RIGHTS INTO THE FOUNDING DOCUMENTS OF THE US

The concept of **natural rights** is engrained in many of America's foundational documents. The Founding Fathers believed that the government exists to protect certain unalienable rights—such as the rights to life, liberty, and property—and they incorporated many of John Locke's theories as they worked to establish a new governmental system. Like Locke before them, the Founders believed these rights to be inherent and felt that they belonged to individuals by virtue of their mere existence. **The Declaration of Independence** (1776), a seminal American document written by Thomas Jefferson, was based heavily on the protection of natural rights, a responsibility that the American colonists believed the British government had failed to uphold. The Declaration of Independence asserts that all people are born with unalienable rights that, if threatened, should serve as justification for rebellion against tyranny. The belief that the British monarchy had failed to adequately protect these rights served as a justification for the American Revolution (1775–1783) and the ultimate creation of an independent American state. Natural rights can also be found in the US Constitution (1787) in a number of locations, including the **First Amendment**, which protects the freedoms of religion, press, speech, and assembly, as well as guaranteeing the right to petition the government. The Founders believed these to be essential inalienable rights that must be protected by the government.

Federalism

OPERATION OF FEDERALISM IN BOTH THEORY AND PRACTICE

Federalism is a system of governance in which power is divided between a national government and a regional government, such as that of a state, region, or province. A federal system is designed to divide power and ensure that each level of government has clearly defined powers and responsibilities. Within such a system, some powers are shared, while others are allocated specifically to one level of government. Typically, the national government in a federal system is responsible for governance of the entirety of the country, while the smaller divisions focus more on local interests and concerns. In the United States, the framers of the Constitution developed a system of **dual sovereignty** in which state governments relinquished a number of their powers to the federal government while retaining others. In accordance with the US Constitution (1787), **enumerated powers**—such as declaring war—are those responsibilities that rest solely with the federal government, while **reserved powers**—including the ability to establish local governments—belong to the state governments. Furthermore, the Constitution also details concurrent powers that belong to both the federal and state governments, such as the ability to tax or make and enforce laws. Ultimately, a federal system works to create a strong central government while also maintaining a degree of state autonomy.

INFLUENCE OF FEDERALISM ON THE DEVELOPMENT OF AMERICAN GOVERNMENT

Federalism is a governmental system in which power is divided between the national and state governments, and it has served an essential role in the development of the US government. After the American colonists gained freedom from the British, the **Articles of Confederation** (1777) served as the first constitution for the newly independent nation, solidifying its position as a sovereign state. The Articles of Confederation established a weak central government and relegated most essential governmental powers to the state governments. The resulting central government lacked the power to raise an army, tax its citizens, or regulate trade, all of which led to a lack of unity and general disorder and, ultimately, to the drafting of the US Constitution in 1787. In the midst of the Constitutional Convention (1788), two separate camps emerged: The Federalists and the Anti-Federalists. The **Federalists**, led by Alexander Hamilton, James Madison, and John Jay, argued that a strong central government that could manage issues at the national level while also respecting the powers of the states was needed for a successful government. The **Anti-Federalists** believed that the proposed Constitution concentrated too much power in the hands of the federal government. The Massachusetts Compromise led to the inclusion of a Bill of Rights to protect both the people and states from a powerful central government, ultimately leading to the ratification of the US Constitution and the establishment of a federal system of government in America.

Individual Liberty

IMPORTANCE OF POLITICAL AND RELIGIOUS LIBERTY TO THE FOUNDERS

Political liberties represented some of the most significant rights to the Founding Fathers. The ability to participate in government through voting and other means, to express opinions regarding the government, and to serve in various political offices, as well as the desire to limit government, all exemplify the value that the Founders placed on political freedoms. Furthermore, the protection of **religious freedoms** was also a priority for the Founding Fathers, who viewed religion as a positive force for the new country that would encourage the virtue and morality required to guide society and promote the public good. That being said, the Founders did not give credence to the notion that the government should support one religious belief or ideology over another, nor did they feel that government should be aligned with any one religious ideology in particular. Therefore, the Founders worked to establish the separation of church and state and to ensure the protection of individual religious freedoms through the addition of the First Amendment to the US Constitution (1787). Ultimately, the tyrannical rule experienced by the colonists under the British monarchy led to the creation of a government built on political and religious liberties.

PROGRESSION OF RELIGIOUS LIBERTY IN US HISTORY

Although many groups, such as the Puritans, traveled to the New World to escape religious persecution at home, the early protection of religious freedom was not always consistent. While some colonies, such as Rhode Island, promoted tolerance, others, like Virginia, established official churches that all citizens of the colony supported through taxation regardless of their religious denomination. The US Constitution (1787) established a clear standard of religious liberty by barring the establishment of a national religion, and it protected against government interference in the religious practices of individuals. This protection did not, however, extend to all religious groups; indigenous peoples, slaves, and Catholics experienced frequent discrimination for their religious views. As time progressed, religious freedom gradually expanded for all sects and denominations. The landmark Supreme Court case ***Everson v The Board of Education*** (1947) interpreted the Establishment Clause of the US Constitution as a means of preventing the funding of religious activity in public schools. Furthermore, the Religious Freedom Restoration Act of 1993 prevents the government from burdening or interfering with an individual's religious practice without a significant reason to do so. Although religious protections in the United States today are far broader than those provided in the period immediately following the ratification of the Constitution, conflicts still arise regarding the scope of such protections.

21

Republicanism and Representative Democratic Government

GUARANTEE OF A REPUBLICAN FORM OF GOVERNMENT FOR EACH STATE

A **republican government** is one in which the people are the ultimate source of power; the people elect officials to develop laws and promote their interests. The US Constitution (1787) guarantees a republican form of government for each state in Article IV, Section 4, which is known as the **Guarantee Clause**. The Guarantee Clause promises that each state in the union will be guaranteed a republican form of government that is protected against invasion. In accordance with this requirement, each state of the union must establish a government that is **representative** in nature, which means power will be vested in the people and the elected officials the people select to represent them in making policy decisions. This ensures that no state is able to develop a dictatorship or other tyrannical form of government where power is concentrated in the hands of a few non-elected officials. Republicanism represents an essential foundational principle of the American governmental system.

ORIGINS OF THE IDEAS OF DEMOCRACY AND THE REPUBLIC

The concepts of democracy and the republic are rooted in ancient Greece and Rome. These principles have evolved over time and played a significant role in the establishment of the American governmental system, as well as in other democratic counties worldwide. Athenian democracy (507–322 BC) is often credited as the first truly democratic system. This system of direct democracy required adult, male citizens over the age of 20 to participate in the assembly that governed the Athenian city-state. These men, known as *demos*, exercised many important rights, such as the freedom of speech, and were active participants in the political process. The Roman Republic (509–27 BC) included elements of democracy alongside more traditional forms of aristocratic governance and comprised three primary branches: the Senate, Magistrates, and Assemblies. Although the Senate held the most power, a system of checks and balances was in place to prevent any one person or branch from becoming too powerful. Members of the Assemblies were Roman citizens that voted directly on policy, while Magistrates were elected officials who held a variety of powers within the Roman government. Ultimately, the principles of democracy and republicanism are evident in the United States' governmental structure and policies and serve an important role in policymaking to this day.

CONTRIBUTION OF ANCIENT CIVILIZATIONS TO MODERN AMERICAN GOVERNMENT

Ancient civilizations, such as Greece and Rome, contributed significantly to the modern-day American government. Greek democracy (507–322 BC), especially that of Athens, promoted the idea of **direct democracy**, a system in which citizens engage directly in the political process. Due to the country's size and general feasibility issues, the United States of America has instituted a **representative democracy** in which citizens elect individuals to make decisions on their behalf; however, the focus on the political participation of the citizenry and the government's resulting accountability to the people connects directly to ancient Greek democracy. That being said, historians often draw connections between a **referendum**, a modern-day political process by which citizens vote directly on an issue or law, and the system of direct democracy exercised in ancient Greece. Furthermore, the general Athenian focus on public debate and civic engagement became an essential component of the American political process. The principle of Roman republicanism also greatly influenced the development of American governmental philosophy. The Roman Republic (509–27 BC) established a **tripartite system of government** in which power was divided between three branches: the Senate, Magistrates, and Assemblies. Power was shared between each branch of government, and a system of checks and balances was in place to ensure that no branch of government became too powerful. The modern American system of government also calls upon a tripartite system to manage governmental operations, and includes the Legislative,

22

Executive, and Judicial Branches. Similar to the Roman model, each branch of the US government has specific powers that can be put into check by the other branches of government. Ultimately, the Founding Fathers relied heavily on early influences as they worked to shape the United States.

REPUBLICAN VS. DEMOCRATIC FORMS OF GOVERNMENT

Although citizens engage in the political process in both republican and democratic governments, the structure and overall exercise of power vary between the two forms. In a **republican government**, citizens elect officials to develop laws and create a governing charter that serves as the basis of government and often protects individual rights. Representatives are accountable to the people and must operate within a framework that limits their overall authority. This helps to ensure that minority rights are not overridden by the majority. In a democratic government, power rests with the people through either a **representative democracy**—in which elected officials make governmental policy based on the needs of their constituents—or **direct democracy**—in which individuals engage directly in the political process by voting on and developing laws. A democracy focuses on the will of the majority, which can result in minority groups losing rights or facing oppression. In true democracies, laws are established by the majority without the same focus on legal constraints prevalent in republics. The United States, like other modern democracies, blends both types of governance by acting as a representative government that operates within the context of a republic and is bound by a constitution.

HOW THE US FUNCTIONS AS A CONSTITUTIONAL REPUBLIC

The United States operates as a **constitutional republic** in which power is granted by a written document that both limits the powers of the government and ensures the protection of its citizens' natural rights. Through this system of governance, citizens elect officials to represent them on the governmental stage. This ensures that the government is representative in nature and that the needs of the citizenry are met and considered when making governmental decisions. In the United States, the US Constitution (1787) provides an outline of the various branches and levels of government as well as of the powers and responsibilities that belong to each. Although the Constitution can be amended or changed, amendments require an arduous process to promote the stability of the government as a whole. **The Bill of Rights**, or the first 10 amendments to the Constitution, allows for the explicit protection of US citizens' natural rights. Ultimately, these attributes help to maintain a constitutional republic where individual rights are valued and governmental power is specifically delineated.

CHARACTERISTICS OF MONARCHIES, DICTATORSHIPS, AND SOCIALIST STATES

Many types of governmental systems exist throughout the world, including monarchies, dictatorships, and socialist states. A **monarchy** is a type of government led by a monarch, such as a king or queen. The monarch typically holds authority for life, and power is transferred based on hereditary succession. Within a monarchy, the source of a leader's power is often believed to be divine. This notion, known as the **divine right of kings**, is based on the belief that the monarch is ordained by God and that it is God's will for that individual to maintain power. Monarchies can be **constitutional**, where power is limited by a constitution or other branches of government, or **absolute**, in which the leader has unlimited power and influence. A **dictatorship** can be similar to a monarchy in that power is often concentrated in the hands of a single individual or small group. In most situations, dictators come to power by force and severely limit the rights of their constituents. Similarly, **socialist states** often control all aspects of government with the purported goal of promoting equitable distribution of wealth. To accomplish this goal, socialist states often nationalize various industries and utilize centralized planning to manage governmental operations.

Constitutionalism

STATE ADHERENCE TO A CONSTITUTIONAL FORM OF GOVERNANCE

A state adheres to a constitutional form of governance when it operates within the confines of a written constitution. Such a constitution should outline the structure of the government and the powers granted to governing authorities. The constitution should be centered around the **rule of law**, a belief that no one, including government officials, is above the law. Furthermore, a constitutional form of government is typically defined by a **separation of power** between different levels and branches of government as well as a system of **checks and balances** that ensures power is not overstepped by any of these branches or levels. A constitutional system also includes provisions for the protection of citizens' natural rights and a predetermined process for amending or changing the constitution. Governments that meet these characteristics and abide by the elements outlined in the constitution can be seen as constitutional in nature.

PHILOSOPHICAL AND PRACTICAL FOUNDATIONS OF CONSTITUTIONALISM

Constitutionalism is built on both philosophical and practical foundations that focus on limiting the power of government, protecting individual rights, and maintaining the rule of law. Philosophies such as **social contract theory**—a principle theorized by John Locke (1632–1704) and Jean-Jacques Rousseau (1712–1778) that views authority as stemming from the consent of the governed—directly support constitutionalism. Constitutionalism also focuses on Baron de Montesquieu's (1689–1755) views on the separation of powers as well as Locke and Immanuel Kant's (1724–1804) philosophies on limited government. In practice, these theories are utilized to establish the framework for constitutionalism. A government based on constitutionalism—such as the government of the United States—not only engrains such philosophies into its governing documents but actively engages in policy choices that promote the fair and equal treatment of its citizens and limit the power of the government overall.

24

Majority Rule, Minority Rights, and Equal Protection

INTERACTION OF MAJORITY RULE WITH THE PROTECTION OF MINORITY RIGHTS

Within democracies, balance must exist between the will of the majority and the rights of the minority. Constitutional protections help to ensure that the majority does not infringe upon minority rights. For example, the Bill of Rights of the US Constitution (1787) protects fundamental rights like the freedoms of speech and religion. This prevents essential freedoms of minority groups from being overridden by majority decisions. Furthermore, the **Equal Protection Clause of the Fourteenth Amendment** guarantees that laws cannot discriminate against minority groups. Based on this clause, states, even those with majority support, are forbidden to treat minority groups unjustly without reason. Historically, the Judicial Branch has been heavily involved in the practical application of this principle. The process of **judicial review** allows the courts to strike down laws and other governmental policies that infringe upon the rights of the minority, even if such policies represent the will of the majority. For example, the landmark Supreme Court case ***Brown v The Board of Education* (1954)** demonstrates how the court can effectively protect the rights of a minority group against the will of the majority. In this case, African American children and families faced state-sanctioned policies of segregation in public schools, and state governments condoned and facilitated this segregation. The Supreme Court ruling in this case—that segregated schools were inherently unequal—represented a real-world application of the Equal Protection Clause.

MEANING AND PRACTICE OF EQUAL PROTECTION

Equal protection, or the notion that all Americans are entitled to the same protections under the law, is enshrined in the US Constitution and promotes the principles of fairness and equity. The most commonly referenced mention of equal protection in the Constitution is found within the **Equal Protection Clause** of the Fourteenth Amendment. This clause mandates that all states must provide individuals within their borders equal protection in similar conditions or circumstances. This ensures that all laws and actions by the state government apply equally to all individuals regardless of race, gender, or other demographic traits. Although the clause was initially ratified in 1868 in a bid to protect the rights of recently freed African Americans, the Supreme Court has since applied the Equal Protection Clause to a wide array of cases, and it is seen as essential to the protection of civil rights in the United States. Ultimately, this application has promoted a lack of discriminatory practices by state governments and, as a result of *Bolling v Sharpe* (1954), national governments as well. Beyond the Fourteenth Amendment, the principle of equal protection was also reinforced by the Fifth Amendment, which requires due process protections for all Americans. These provisions guarantee equal protection as a foundational philosophy within American democracy and require fair treatment of all citizens in the eyes of the law.

25

Bill of Rights and the Protections of Civil Rights and Liberties

HOW THE BILL OF RIGHTS PROTECTS THE INDIVIDUAL RIGHTS OF US CITIZENS

The Bill of Rights, or the first 10 amendments to the United States Constitution (1787), serves an essential role within United States democracy by limiting the power of the government and safeguarding the rights of the people. Written in 1789 and ratified in 1791, the authors of the Bill of Rights sought to ensure the protection of the citizenry against a powerful central government. The **First Amendment** ensures that basic rights such as freedom of religion, press, and speech are not infringed upon by the government, while the **Second Amendment** protects the right to bear arms. The Bill of Rights was also intended to prevent general governmental overreach and to identify procedures that must be followed. For example, the **Fifth Amendment** guarantees a number of procedural protections, such as the right to a grand jury and the protection against self-incrimination. Finally, the Bill of Rights guarantees fairness in legal proceedings, with the **Sixth Amendment** ensuring that the accused have the right to counsel, a speedy trial, and an impartial jury. Ultimately, The Bill of Rights forbids the government from infringing upon individual freedoms, and it allows citizens to challenge unlawful or unfair governmental actions.

ROLE OF THE SUPREME COURT IN INTERPRETING THE SAFEGUARDS AND LIMITATIONS

The Supreme Court plays an important role in interpreting the Bill of Rights to ensure that its protections are applied consistently across the United States. Through **judicial review**, the Supreme Court is able to determine the constitutionality of the actions of each branch of government. This helps to protect the rights of US citizens and to establish important legal precedents to guide related decisions in the future. Furthermore, the court applies freedoms included in the Bill of Rights to modern issues. For example, in *Tinker v Des Moines* **(1969)**, the Supreme Court expanded the scope of the First Amendment when it ruled that students do not lose their constitutional rights by virtue of their enrollment in public schools. The Supreme Court also expanded on the protections offered by the Bill of Rights through the landmark case *Gitlow v New York* **(1925)**. In *Gitlow v New York*, the justices ruled that, through the **incorporation doctrine**, most components of the first 10 amendments apply to state governments in addition to the federal government. The Supreme Court allows the protections of the Bill of Rights to be upheld while evolving to meet the needs of a changing populace.

HOW LIBERTIES PROVIDED UNDER THE BILL OF RIGHTS MIGHT BE LIMITED

Although the Bill of Rights protects the civil liberties of US citizens, certain situations require such liberties to be limited. For example, the **First Amendment** provides protections for the freedom of speech; however, limitations may be put into place when speech is used to incite violence or for other obscene and defamatory behaviors. Furthermore, the **Second Amendment** safeguards the right to bear arms. This right is limited by requiring background checks or refusing gun ownership to convicted felons. Finally, the due process protections provided under the **Fifth Amendment** may be limited during times of war, in which case an individual may be detained without a trial. While these limitations are allowed in certain circumstances, it is important to note that they must be justified and that their application be limited in scope to maintain an overall protection of the Bill of Rights and its safeguards. When considering limitations on the civil liberties included in the Bill of Rights, it is important to note that various branches of government may enact them. For example, the Supreme Court may determine that an individual's speech is not protected by the First Amendment if the speech was used to encourage a violent protest. Additionally, per the US Constitution (1787), Congress or the President can suspend **habeas corpus**, or the protection against unlawful detainment or imprisonment, in an emergency situation.

Elections

IMPORTANCE OF FREE, FAIR AND SECURE ELECTIONS

Free, fair, and secure elections are essential components of any democratic society, as they help guarantee that officials voted into office are representative of the will of the people and have not been put into place by non-democratic means. A **free election** allows each citizen to engage in the voting process without encountering any barriers, such as intimidation or forced fees. A **fair election** guarantees that each vote cast carries the same weight and includes measures that work against voter fraud and bias. Fair elections promote the belief amongst the populace that their vote matters and that election results are reflective of the choices of the people as a whole. Finally, **secure elections** ensure each vote is accurately counted and that no outside interference occurs in relation to the casting or tallying of ballots. These principles help to promote trust in governmental institutions as well as ensure accountability of elected officials to the public.

HOW ELECTIONS OPERATE AT THE FEDERAL LEVEL

Federal elections are held for members of Congress (US House of Representatives and US Senate) and the President and Vice President. Elections for the President and Vice President are held every four years on the first Tuesday after the first Monday of November. Although voters cast their ballot in the popular vote, they are actually voting for electors to the **Electoral College** who have pledged support for a particular set of candidates. Each state has a predetermined number of electors based on the total population of the state. In most cases, the candidate who wins the popular vote in a state receives all of the electoral votes for that state. In order to win the presidency, a candidate must attain the majority of the electoral votes, or 270 out of 435. Congressional elections, on the other hand, occur every two years, with senators serving six-year terms and members of the House serving two-year terms. The President of the United States is subject to a two-year term limit as a result of the **Twenty-second Amendment**, while members of Congress may serve unlimited terms in office. Elections for both Houses of Congress are based on the popular vote, with senators elected statewide and members of the House of Representatives elected from congressional districts. Many federal and state guidelines exist to ensure fair and equitable voting on Election Day.

HOW ELECTIONS OPERATE AT THE STATE LEVEL

While there are some minor state variations, elections at the state level are generally held for the governor, state legislators, and local officials. State elections typically follow the schedule for federal elections and occur on the first Tuesday after the first Monday of November. Elections for lower-level local officials may be held at various times throughout the year depending on need and local voting guidelines. Terms vary for state officials across the United States, and elections are held in accordance with pre-determined terms and election day policies. The results of state elections are based on **popular vote**, meaning that the candidate who receives the highest number of votes wins the election. This is in direct contrast to the election of the President of the United States, who is elected by the **Electoral College**. Although voters in the federal voting system cast their ballots for the presidential candidate in the popular vote, they are actually voting for electors to the Electoral College who have pledged support for a particular set of candidates. Beyond voting for officials, some states allow citizens to engage in a **referendum** by voting to approve laws or changes to the state constitution. Overall, each state establishes its own policy for the voting process, including guidelines for voting itself and for absentee ballots, early voting provisions, and voter registration.

27

The United States Constitution and Its Application

Articles

ORGANIZATION OF THE US CONSTITUTION

The US Constitution (1787) represents the primary foundational document of the United States. The Constitution is organized into eight sections: a preamble which introduces the general purpose of the document and then seven articles that each describe the powers, responsibilities, and structure of the government. Each article is broken down into sections, and sometimes clauses, which allows for better overall organization and clarity when reading the document. Additionally, 27 amendments, including those considered to fall under the Bill of Rights, have been made to the Constitution. These modifications further define the individual freedoms of the people of the United States, and they also clarify the relationship between the state and federal governments and between the people and the government overall. The Constitution, and the system of the US government in general, has been emulated by democracies around the world and serves as a guide for the development of a republican form of government.

CHARACTERISTICS OF THE PREAMBLE OF THE US CONSTITUTION

The **Preamble** of the US Constitution (1787) serves as the introduction to the document and details its overall purpose and goals. The Preamble begins with the phrase "We the People," which establishes the tone of the Constitution and highlights one of the primary goals of the framers: developing a system of governance based on **popular sovereignty**, in which power derives from the people themselves. Furthermore, the Preamble establishes the importance of liberty, justice, and peace, as well as unity among the states. Although the Preamble is not a law in and of itself, it helps those reading and analyzing the document to understand who is developing the document and for what purpose.

CONTENTS OF ARTICLE I OF THE US CONSTITUTION

Article I of the US Constitution (1787) establishes the **Legislative Branch** and outlines its responsibilities and powers. Furthermore, Article I grants all legislative power to the US Congress, which includes both the **US Senate** and **US House of Representatives**. Both Houses are detailed at length, including qualifications, term length, compensation, and election protocol of those serving in office in either chamber, as well as apportionment of seats for the House and the role of the Vice President as the President of the Senate. Additionally, Article I explains the process by which lawmaking takes place, including the passage of bills and the ability of the President of the United States to veto or override legislation with which he or she disagrees. Article I also outlines the enumerated powers, or those powers explicitly granted to Congress and the federal government, as well as limitations on the power of both Congress and state governments. Ultimately, Article I represents the longest article in the Constitution, demonstrating the importance placed on the Legislative Branch by the framers.

SECTIONS I–V OF ARTICLE I OF THE US CONSTITUTION

Article I of the US Constitution establishes the Legislative Branch and is broken into 10 sections that detail the branch's powers and limitations. The first five sections deal primarily with the establishment of the branch, necessary qualifications of representatives, and general operating procedures.

- **Section I** develops a **bicameral**, or two-house, legislature that is made up of a Senate and House of Representatives. All legislative power rests with these two Houses.
- **Section II** explains the characteristics of the House of Representatives. It details the way in which representation is apportioned based on the population of the state. It also provides an overview of qualifications required to serve in the House and rules for the election of such individuals. Furthermore, the House is designated as the legislative body that is able to vote to impeach an individual.
- **Section III** establishes the Senate and dictates that each state will have two senators who will serve six-year terms each. Each senator must meet certain qualifications, such as being at least 30 years of age and having held US citizenship for a minimum of nine years. This section also designates the Vice President of the United States as President of the Senate. Furthermore, this section describes the role of the Senate in impeachment hearings for those impeached by the House of Representatives.
- **Section IV** empowers the states to set the time and place of elections with the potential for Congressional oversight. Additionally, this section requires that Congress meet at least once per year at a regular time.
- **Section V** reviews the general operating procedures of Congress. Each House is responsible for the conduct and elections of its members. Members of both Houses are responsible for developing rules to guide their daily operations and must maintain logs of what they say and do during a session in most cases. Section V also forbids one House of Congress from adjourning for longer than three days, unless both Houses decide to do so.

SECTIONS VI–X OF ARTICLE I OF THE US CONSTITUTION

Article I of the US Constitution establishes the Legislative Branch and is broken into 10 sections that detail the branch's powers and limitations. Sections VI through X focus primarily on the powers and limitations of Congress, as well as the process by which a bill is passed.

- **Section VI** details the required terms of pay, as well as privileges and immunities for officials serving in the Legislative Branch. Additionally, this section establishes that those elected to office are not permitted to serve in another governmental position concurrently.
- **Section VII** reviews the process for passing laws as well as the role of the President of the United States in signing bills into law. The process by which the President may **veto**, or override, bills passed by Congress is also reviewed.
- **Section VIII** lists the specific powers of Congress, including taxation, declarations of war, regulation of commerce, and maintenance of the nation's armed forces.
- **Section IX** reviews the limitations placed on Congress' power, such as the inability to suspend **Habeas Corpus**, or the requirement that the government must demonstrate reasonable cause in a courtroom to detain an individual, except in cases of foreign invasion or rebellion.

Section X restricts the powers of the states. For example, in accordance with this section, states may not wage war, coin their own money, or develop treaties.

COMPONENTS OF ARTICLE II OF THE US CONSTITUTION

Article II of the US Constitution (1787) pertains to the **Executive Branch** of the United States Government. The Executive Branch is responsible for the administration and enforcement of laws. Overall, Article II outlines the powers and responsibilities of both the President and the Vice President of the United States, and it comprises four sections.

- **Section I** vests executive power in the President and establishes the office of the Vice President. Additionally, this section outlines the process by which the Electoral College is used to elect the President. Section I also details the qualifications required of the President, rules for presidential succession, compensation information, and the required oath of office.
- **Section II** explains presidential powers and includes the Commander in Chief Clause, which recognizes the President as the commander of the nation's armed forces. This second section of Article II also identifies the power of the President to pardon individuals who have been accused of federal offenses, as well as the President's ability to establish a cabinet, negotiate treaties with the consent of the Senate, and appoint important officials.
- **Section III** expands on the duties of the President, such as the responsibility of delivering a State of the Union Address, receiving ambassadors, and ensuring the faithful execution of laws. This third section of Article II also highlights the ability of the President to call Congress into session.
- **Section IV** explains the process by which the President and other elected officials can be impeached, or removed from office, if found guilty of the offenses of bribery, treason, or other serious legal violations.

ARTICLE III OF THE US CONSTITUTION

Article III of the US Constitution (1787) establishes the **Judicial Branch**. The ability to interpret the law, as well as to determine if laws and other actions violate the Constitution, rests with the Judicial Branch. Organized into three sections, Article III details the federal judicial system and explains its overall structure as well as the powers and responsibilities of the courts.

- **Section I** establishes judicial authority in the Supreme Court and grants Congress the ability to establish lower courts. Office terms for federal judges are also outlined in Section I, which states these judges are eligible to serve for life given "good behavior."
- **Section II** explains the **jurisdiction**, or the authority of a court to hear and make legal decisions on a case. In accordance with Section II, federal courts have jurisdiction over cases pertaining to Constitution or federal law, cases dealing with foreign ambassadors, issues on international waters, lawsuits against the United States, and disputes between citizens of different states. The original and appellate jurisdiction of the Supreme Court is also detailed. Finally, Section II explains that all federal trials will be jury trials and will be heard in the state in which the crime was committed, except in the case of impeachment hearings.
- **Section III** defines **treason** as a betrayal against the United States that may include waging war against the US or showing loyalty or support to an enemy of the state. In order to be convicted of treason, two or more witnesses must detail the act in court, or the accused must confess. In accordance with Section III, Congress has the power to determine the punishment for treasonous behavior.

ARTICLE IV OF THE US CONSTITUTION

Article IV provides an overview of the relationship between the federal and state governments and is organized into four separate sections.

- **Section I** includes the **Full Faith and Credit Clause**, which dictates that each state must recognize the public records and acts as well as judicial proceedings of each state. Congress has the ability to oversee and test state records for effectiveness.
- **Section II** includes two important clauses: the **Privileges and Immunities Clause**, which ensures that citizens from each state have the same rights as citizens from other states, and the **Extradition Clause**, which mandates that an individual charged with a crime that flees to another state must be extradited, or returned to the state where the crime occurred.
- **Section III** provides Congress with the power to admit new states into the union, and it prevents the forming of new states from the land of another without the permission of Congress and the legislature of the state in question. Additionally, Section III provides Congress with the power to develop laws and regulations for any federal territories or lands of the United States.
- **Section IV** guarantees that each state in the union has a **republican** form of government in which officials are elected by the citizens. Additionally, this section offers states protection from attacks and from localized fighting and rebellion.

ARTICLE V OF THE US CONSTITUTION

Article V of the United States Constitution (1787) explains the process of amending the document to best meet the needs of a changing country.

In accordance with Article V, amendments can be proposed in two different ways:

- Congress can propose an amendment as a result of a two-thirds majority vote in both the US Senate and the US House of Representatives.
- An amendment can also be proposed when two-thirds of state legislatures (34 states) vote to convene a convention to propose an amendment.

Upon proposal, the amendment must be ratified using one of two measures:

- Three-quarters of state legislatures (38 states) vote to ratify the amendment.
- Three-quarters of state conventions (38 states) vote to ratify the amendment.

With the amendment process, the framers of the Constitution sought to develop a system that, although relatively straightforward and open to the changing needs of the United States, ensured that the document would not be modified for frivolous reasons that did not reflect the will of the majority.

United States Constitution

31

ARTICLE VI OF THE US CONSTITUTION

Article VI of the US Constitution (1787) covers a variety of topics, including supremacy, oaths, and governmental debts. This article is organized into three clauses.

- **Clause I** details that any debt or promise made prior to the adoption of the Constitution must be upheld.
- **Clause II** is known as the **Supremacy Clause** and explains that the Constitution, plus any federal legislation, serves as the supreme law of the land and supersedes any state laws.
- **Clause III** requires that all elected officials swear an oath of office in which they promise to uphold the Constitution. Additionally, Clause III prevents the use of any religious test as a requirement for public office.

ARTICLE VII OF THE US CONSTITUTION

Article VII explains the overall process by which the United States Constitution (1787) would be ratified. At the time of the Constitution's ratification, only 13 states were in existence. Article VII required that at least 9 out of the 13 states vote to adopt the Constitution. This was in direct contrast to the **Articles of Confederation** (1777), which required all 13 states to ratify the document before it became law. Also included within Article VII is the signature of George Washington, President and Deputy from Virginia, as well as the delegates of the 12 states that originally signed the document: Delaware, North Carolina, New Hampshire, New Jersey, Maryland, South Carolina, Massachusetts, Pennsylvania, Georgia, Connecticut, and New York).

AMENDMENT SECTION OF THE US CONSTITUTION

The amendments represent the third and final section of the United States Constitution (1787) and include the various changes that have been made to the foundational American governmental document. Overall, the Constitution has been amended 27 times, starting with the Bill of Rights in 1791. Some framers of the Constitution argued that a bill of rights protecting individual liberties was not necessary, as the government could only exercise those powers it was granted. However, others, such as George Mason, refused to sign the Constitution without a bill of rights. The promised consideration of a bill of rights led to the ultimate signing and ratification of the Constitution. When added, the Bill of Rights represented the first 10 amendments to the US Constitution. The remaining 17 amendments sought to make changes to the framework and operations of the US government as American society evolved, and those amendments expanded the protections offered under the Bill of Rights and other Constitutional provisions to all US citizens, regardless of race or sex.

EXPRESSED VS. IMPLIED POWERS IN THE US CONSTITUTION

Article I Section VIII of the United States Constitution (1787) details the powers granted to the US Congress. Congress is generally understood to have two primary types of powers: **expressed** and **implied**. Expressed powers are sometimes referred to as **enumerated** or **delegated** powers. These powers are explicitly listed in the Constitution and include actions such as regulating commerce, taxing, raising an army, and coining money. Conversely, **implied powers** are those that, although they are not directly listed in the Constitution, have been interpreted to belong to Congress through the **Necessary and Proper Clause**. The Necessary and Proper Clause grants Congress the powers to develop laws that are needed to carry out its expressed powers. For example, Congress justified its decision to establish a national minimum wage in 1938 through the Necessary and Proper Clause, as well as its ability to regulate commerce. Ultimately, expressed powers are those written directly in the Constitution, while implied powers are those that have been interpreted over time to belong to the Legislative Branch.

32

Amendments and Selective Incorporation

HOW AN AMENDMENT IS ADDED TO THE US CONSTITUTION

A two-step process that includes proposal and ratification is required to add an amendment or make a change to the US Constitution (1787). This process is outlined in Article V of the Constitution.

- **Proposal**: An amendment can be proposed in one of two ways.
  1. Two-thirds of the United States Congress vote to propose an amendment to the Constitution.
  2. Two-thirds of state legislatures (34 states) request a convention where the amendment will be proposed. This option has never been utilized.
- **Ratification:** Following the proposal of an amendment it must be ratified or approved. This can occur in one of two ways.
  1. Three-quarters of state legislatures (38 states) vote to ratify the amendment.
  2. Three-quarters of states vote to ratify the amendment at individual state-based legislatures. This method has only been utilized for the ratification of the 21st amendment.

Upon ratification, the amendment officially becomes part of the US Constitution.

BILL OF RIGHTS AND LATER AMENDMENTS

IMPORTANCE OF THE BILL OF RIGHTS

The first ten amendments of the US Constitution are known as the **Bill of Rights**. These amendments prevent the government from infringing upon certain freedoms that the Founding Fathers believed were natural rights that already belonged to all people. These rights included freedom of speech, freedom of religion, freedom of assembly, and the right to bear arms. Many of these rights were formulated in direct response to the way the colonists felt they had been mistreated by the British government.

RIGHTS GRANTED IN THE BILL OF RIGHTS

The first ten amendments were passed by Congress in 1789. Three-quarters of the existing thirteen states had ratified them by December of 1791, making them official additions to the Constitution. The rights granted in the Bill of Rights are:

- **First Amendment:** freedom of religion, freedom of speech, freedom of the press, and the right to assemble and to petition the government
- **Second Amendment:** the right to bear arms
- **Third Amendment:** prevents Congress from forcing individuals to house troops
- **Fourth Amendment:** protection from unreasonable search and seizure
- **Fifth Amendment:** protects individuals from being required to testify against themselves and from being tried twice for the same crime
- **Sixth Amendment:** the right to criminal trial by jury and the right to legal counsel
- **Seventh Amendment:** the right to civil trial by jury
- **Eighth Amendment:** protection from excessive bail or cruel and unusual punishment

United States Constitution

33

- **Ninth Amendment:** prevents rights not explicitly named in the Constitution from being taken away because they are not named
- **Tenth Amendment:** clarifies that any rights not directly delegated to the national government, or not directly prohibited by the government from the states, belong to the states or to the people

---

Review Video: Bill of Rights
Visit mometrix.com/academy and enter code: 585149

The United States Constitution (1787) has been amended 27 times since its inception. Amendments 11–19 of the Constitution cover a number of different topics ranging from voting rights to the powers of the Judicial Branch.

- **Eleventh Amendment (1795):** prevents federal courts from hearing cases in which a state is sued by individuals from another country or state (This protection is known as sovereign immunity.)
- **Twelfth Amendment (1804):** explains the process for electing the President and Vice President and includes the provision that electors have two separate ballots: one for the President and one for the Vice President
- **Thirteenth Amendment (1865):** bans the practice of slavery in the United States and states that no individual can be forced to work without pay, unless as a form of punishment for an individual who has been convicted of a crime in a court of law
- **Fourteenth Amendment (1868):** grants the same rights as all other US citizens to any individual who is born in the United States or who gains citizenship and specifies that these rights cannot be taken away by any state
- **Fifteenth Amendment (1870):** declares that an individual cannot be denied the right to vote based upon skin color, race, or previous position as a slave
- **Sixteenth Amendment (1913):** provides Congress the power to levy taxes without basing that tax on population of the states
- **Seventeenth Amendment (1913):** allows for the direct election of US senators based upon the popular vote and not the vote of state legislatures
- **Eighteenth Amendment (1919):** banned the manufacturing, distribution, and sale of alcohol across the United States, beginning the period known as Prohibition
- **Nineteenth Amendment (1920):** prevents the government from restricting voting rights on the basis of gender

The United States Constitution (1787) has been amended 27 times in total. Amendments 20–27 cover a variety of topics, including individual rights and governmental procedures.

- **Twentieth Amendment (1933):** reduced the period of time between the presidential election and the start of the new term, limiting the "**lame duck**" period of the presidency
- **Twenty-First Amendment (1933):** repealed the Eighteenth Amendment and ended the period of prohibition in the United States
- **Twenty-Second Amendment (1951):** limits the time the President can serve in office to no more than two terms
- **Twenty-Third Amendment (1961):** provided residents of Washington DC with the right to vote and granted them three electoral votes
- **Twenty-Fourth Amendment (1964):** banned the use of poll taxes in federal elections, ultimately reducing voting discrimination based on wealth

- **Twenty-Fifth Amendment (1967):** set up procedures for presidential succession and outlined the protocol for instances of presidential incapacitation
- **Twenty-Sixth Amendment (1971):** reduced the voting age to 18 in all federal and state elections
- **Twenty-Seventh Amendment (1992):** prevented congressional representatives from increasing their compensation until after the next election.

IMPACT OF AMENDMENTS ON CIVIC PARTICIPATION OVER TIME

Amendments to the US Constitution have played a major role in promoting civic participation. Civic participation can be understood as the way Americans engage in local, state, and federal government, and it may include acts such as voting, connecting with elected officials, registering voters, and volunteering at polling places. In general, a successful democracy relies on participation by its citizens. Civic participation ensures that the voice of the people is heard and considered within the political process, which in turn ensures that the will of the majority wins without crushing minority opinions and concerns. The **Fifteenth** and **Nineteenth** Amendments provided all US citizens with the right to vote regardless of race (Fifteenth Amendment) or gender (Nineteenth Amendment); these amendments increased the overall size of the electorate. Similarly, the **Twenty-Fourth Amendment** banned the use of poll taxes, a fee required to vote in some jurisdictions, and reduced discriminatory practices that often prevented low-income citizens, especially recently free enslaved persons, from exercising their right to vote. This measure further increased voting access and overall political participation across the United States. The **Twenty-Sixth Amendment** served as a final change designed to increase participation in US elections and civic engagement in general by reducing the voting age from 21 to 18 years of age. Ultimately, these amendments help to ensure a more representative democratic process in which elected officials better serve the will of the populace.

HOW AMENDMENTS HAVE CHANGED US GOVERNMENT AND SOCIETY OVER TIME

Amendments to the United States Constitution have brought about significant changes to US government through the expansion of rights to all US citizens and modifications to overall governmental structure and procedures. Amendments **Thirteen**, **Fourteen**, and **Fifteen** worked to promote equality and freedom for all Americans by banning slavery (Thirteenth), granting citizenship rights for freed slaves (Fourteenth), and ensuring equal rights regardless of skin color or prior history of enslavement. Several amendments have also brought about changes within the government itself. The **Twenty-Second Amendment** limited the presidential term to a maximum of two four-year terms. Although this precedent was established by America's first President, George Washington (1732–1799), the decision of President Franklin Delano Roosevelt (1882–1945) to seek a third term encouraged Congress to formally establish the policy on term limits. Additionally, the **Twenty-Fifth Amendment** also pertains to the operations of the government, as it details the process of presidential succession. If the President is found to be unable to fulfil the required duties, then, with the approval of Congress, the Vice President can take on the position. This ensures continuity in the leadership of the Executive Branch. Ultimately, these amendments work together to guarantee a government that promotes both equality and smooth governmental operations.

HOW AMENDMENTS APPLY TO BOTH FEDERAL AND STATE GOVERNMENTS

The amendments apply to both federal and state governments. Originally, the **Bill of Rights**, or the first 10 amendments of the US Constitution, applied to only the federal government, while the constitutions of state governments were expected to have their own bills of rights; however, the **Fourteenth Amendment** changed this expectation. The Fourteenth Amendment provides equal protection to all foreign- and natural-born citizens of the United States and prevents states from treating their citizens in an inequitable manner. Two important clauses within the Fourteenth Amendment ensure the application of all amendments at the state level: the **Due Process Clause** and the **Equal Protection Clause**. The Due Process Clause prevents the government from infringing upon an individual's freedom without due process, or through the use of fair procedures and legal processes. The Supreme Court has utilized a process known as s**elective incorporation** to apply the Bill of Rights to the states and prevent infringement of civil liberties through the Fourteenth Amendment. The Equal Protection Clause prevents any state from denying individuals within its borders equal protection under the law. The Supreme Court has applied this clause to prevent discriminatory processes by the states, such as the segregation of public schools. Overall, the Fourteenth Amendment has served as a powerful tool and has been used to promote equality across the United States.

Federalists vs Anti-Federalists

ARGUMENTS AGAINST THE RATIFICATION OF THE US CONSTITUTION

Those against the ratification of the United States Constitution (1787) were known as Anti-Federalists. Anti-Federalists such as Patrick Henry, Richard Henry Lee, and George Mason had several concerns regarding the Constitution.

- **Strength of the central government:** Anti-Federalists worried that too much power was concentrated in the hands of the federal government at the expense of state governments. Much of the authority that originally belonged to state governments under the Articles of Confederation (1777) was transferred to the federal government under the Constitution. Anti-Federalists feared that a powerful executive branch could lead to tyranny and that the Necessary and Proper Clause gave Congress the potential for unchecked power by the federal government.
- **Lack of a Bill of Rights:** A Bill of Rights listing specific protections of the civil liberties of Americans was not included in the original Constitution. Anti-Federalists feared that, without such an inclusion, a powerful government could emulate that of the British Crown and infringe upon the rights of the citizenry.
- **Representative nature of the government:** Anti-Federalists expressed concern that a representative form of government, in which elected officials governed on behalf of the people, could become detached from the true will of the people. They supported a more direct level of involvement by citizens. Furthermore, the Anti-Federalists were fearful of the Senate's lack of election through more direct means and that its lack of proportionality based on population would lead to unfair representation.

Ultimately, the Anti-Federalists feared that the Constitution would lead to a centralized government that was too powerful and that would not be reactive to the will of the people.

ARGUMENTS IN FAVOR OF THE RATIFICATION OF THE US CONSTITUTION

Those in favor of the ratification of the United States Constitution (1787) were known as **Federalists**. The Federalists, led by Alexander Hamilton, John Jay, and James Madison, argued that the Constitution represented the best path forward for the new country. They felt that the Constitution met the need for a stronger central government. The previous governing document, the **Articles of Confederation** (1777), created a weak central government and powerful state governments. This system resulted in a variety of problems, such as the inability of the central government to solve interstate debates or raise taxes. Federalists believed that the Constitution would establish a system of governance known as **federalism**, in which power was divided between the federal and state governments. Although states would retain a number of powers and

responsibilities, the federal government would yield the most power; Federalists believed that this was a necessity in promoting economic and political stability. Furthermore, the Federalists believed that the Constitution established an effective system of **checks and balances** in which each branch—Executive, Judicial, and Legislative—has the ability to limit the power of another. The Federalists argued that checks and balances coupled with federalism would prevent tyranny and the abuse of power and would promote a system of governance that would withstand the test of time.

Clauses of the United States Constitution

SUPREMACY CLAUSE

The **Supremacy Clause** can be found in Article VI, Clause II of the United States Constitution (1787). It states that the Constitution and all federal laws and treaties supersede those of any state and represent the supreme law of the land. In situations where federal and state law conflict, federal law presides. This principle can be seen through the process of **judicial review**, in which the Supreme Court determines if state policy is in violation of the Constitution. Overall, the Supremacy Clause helps to maintain a sense of consistency across the United States and ensures that state laws do not violate or contradict those of the federal government.

NECESSARY AND PROPER CLAUSE

The **Necessary and Proper Clause** is located in Article I, Section VIII, Clause XVIII of the US Constitution (1787). Also known as the **Elastic Clause**, the Necessary and Proper Clause allows Congress to make any law deemed "necessary and proper" to carry out the enumerate powers specifically designated in the Constitution. This provision allows Congressional power to grow and to handle issues not specifically mentioned in the Constitution. Since the Supreme Court ruling in *McCulloch v Maryland* (1819), this clause has been interpreted to include implied powers, or those not specifically mentioned in the Constitution but deemed necessary. For example, in *McCulloch v Maryland*, the Court ruled that Congress had the power to establish a bank because a bank assists with the enumerated power of taxation. Although the Necessary and Proper Clause has faced controversy for its ability to provide Congress with broad powers, it has ultimately allowed the federal government to meet the needs of a changing nation.

EQUAL PROTECTION CLAUSE

The **Equal Protection Clause** can be found in the **Fourteenth Amendment** of the US Constitution (1787) and requires each state to treat those in its jurisdiction fairly under the law. Although the intent of the clause was to protect the rights of recently freed slaves residing in the southern states, it has since been used to prevent discrimination on a number of levels. The Equal Protection Clause has been applied to a number of different cases by the Supreme Court. For example, the clause served as a basis of *Brown v Board of Education* **(1954)** to stop racial segregation in public schools, and again in *United States v Virginia* **(1996)** to promote gender equality in education. Ultimately, the Equal Protection Clause has consistently been applied to reduce discriminatory practices across the United States.

COMMERCE CLAUSE

The **Commerce Clause** can be found in Article I, Section III, Clause VIII of the US Constitution (1787). This clause grants Congress the power to regulate commerce within the United States, as well as with foreign states. The Commerce Clause has provided the federal government with significant power to engage in and regulate a number of economic activities, including those pertaining to the labor and transportation industries. Furthermore, the Commerce Clause has been

37

United States Constitution

used to justify wide-scale regulatory measures outside of the typical understanding of the term commerce. For example, the Commerce Clause was used as a basis for the **Affordable Care Act (2010)**, which requires all Americans to purchase health insurance and face additional taxation if they fail to do so, and the **Civil Rights Act of 1964**, which prevents discrimination in public accommodations that are related to interstate commerce. Ultimately, the Commerce Clause has allowed Congress to engage in the regulation of economic activities that have national impacts.

DUE PROCESS CLAUSE

The **Due Process Clause** can be found in both the Fifth and Fourteenth Amendment to the United States Constitution (1787). This clause ensures that neither the federal (Fifth Amendment) nor state (Fourteenth Amendment) governments can deprive an individual's life, liberty, or property without following a predetermined legal process. Both **procedural** (promoting equitable procedures such as a fair trial) and **substantive** (protecting important rights from governmental intrusion) due process are guaranteed by the Due Process Clause. The Supreme Court has applied and interpreted the Due Process Clause in a number of important decisions. For example, in *Griswold v Connecticut* **(1965)**, the Supreme Court applied the Due Process Clause in ruling that the Constitution protects American's right to privacy, including an individual's choice to utilize contraception. Overall, the Supreme Court has called upon the Due Process Clause to cover new rights that apply to all US citizens.

Founding Documents and How They Have Shaped the Nature and Functions of Our Institutions of Self-Government

Declaration of Independence

The **Declaration of Independence** was signed by the leadership of each of the 13 American colonies on July 4, 1776. The colonies' lack of representation in British Parliament, combined with unfair taxation policy and British occupancy of the colonies, compelled the colonists to formally declare independence from Great Britain and establish the United States of America as a sovereign nation free from imperial rule. The document relies heavily on Enlightenment ideals and outlined the importance of certain natural rights belonging to all people. Additionally, the document details the grievances carried out by King George III of England. Organized into five separate sections—introduction, preamble, indictment of King George III, denunciation of the British people, and the conclusion—the Declaration of Independence sought to serve as a justification for the American Revolution (1775–1783). Ultimately, the Declaration of Independence serves as a foundational document in US history, one that reiterates the core values of American democracy.

INFLUENCE OF ENLIGHTENMENT IDEALS ON THE DECLARATION OF INDEPENDENCE

The Declaration of Independence (1776) was heavily influenced by Enlightenment ideals. **The Enlightenment** (1685–1815) was an era of significant change in which intellectuals focused on rational thought, science, and reason to explain the world around them and to promote change in governance and the social order in general. When drafting the Declaration of Independence, Thomas Jefferson (1743–1826) and the other contributing authors drew primarily from the theories of **John Locke (1632–1704)** a prominent Enlightenment thinker in their focus on natural rights and the right to revolution. In his book *Two Treatises of Government* (1689), John Locke explains that all humans have natural rights that the government is required to protect. According to Locke, if the government fails to protect these rights, the people have a right and responsibility to overthrow the government and replace it with one that is accountable to the people. Jefferson referenced these views throughout the Declaration of Independence as a justification for an American revolution against the British Crown. Furthermore, the idea of social contract theory, a theory developed by Locke, Thomas Hobbes (1588–1679), and Jean-Jacques Rousseau (1712–1778) is incorporated into the Declaration of Independence. Social contract theory—or the idea that people give up some of their rights in order to be protected by the government that represents the will of the people—can be found in the preamble and throughout the Constitution. The preamble starts with the famous phrase "We the People," indicating that the people themselves serve as a power source for the government. Various statements throughout the document then emphasize the government's responsibility to protect the natural rights of the people. Ultimately, the Enlightenment served as an essential influence for the authors of the Declaration of Independence.

DOCUMENTS INFLUENCING THE DECLARATION OF INDEPENDENCE

The Declaration of Independence was drafted in 1776 to detail the colonists' decision to formally break free from Great Britain, as well as to outline their reasons for doing so. The document represents an important foundational document for the United States government and was influenced by a variety of sources.

- **Magna Carta (1215):** The Magna Carta, or Great Charter, sought to limit the power of the King of England and ensure that he and his representatives were subject to the same laws as all British citizens. This was the first document to formally establish this notion of the rule of law, and it was signed by King John of England. The Magna Carta also provided for the protection of a number of individual rights, such as due process, and certain property rights. As individuals of British descent, the colonists were familiar with the Magna Carta, and they felt that its provisions should apply to them and offer them protection against unfair treatment by the British Crown.
- **English Bill of Rights (1689):** The English Bill of Rights further limited the power of the British monarchy. It detailed the protection of natural rights and provided Englishmen the right to petition the government. The colonists felt that the English Bill of Rights applied to them as Englishmen themselves, and they incorporated these aspects of the English Bill of Rights throughout the document when drafting the Declaration of Independence.
- ***Second Treatise of Government* (1689):** Written by John Locke, the *Second Treatise of Government* outlines his **social contract theory**, which argues that citizens give up some of their natural rights in exchange for protection by the government. Furthermore, the *Second Treatise of Government* argues that the government derives its power through the consent of the governed and that the people have the right and responsibility to overthrow the government if it does not protect their rights. These principles directly shaped the arguments included in the Declaration of Independence.

The ideals presented in these documents greatly influenced the colonists not only in their development of the Declaration of Independence, but also in the creation of the United States' governmental system in general.

IDEALS INCLUDED IN THE DECLARATION OF INDEPENDENCE

When the **Declaration of Independence** was drafted in 1776, it included a number of principles that served as the foundation for the establishment of a constitutional republic in the United States.

- **Natural Rights:** The Declaration of Independence focused on the protection of certain unalienable rights that belonged to all men regardless of various socioeconomic factors. The Declaration promised to protect the life, liberty, and pursuit of happiness of all Americans. This notion is engrained in the US constitutional republic today and serves as an essential foundational principle that continues to guide governmental actions.
- **Popular Sovereignty:** The Declaration asserts that the power of the government is derived from the people. Popular sovereignty serves as yet another foundational ideal evident in the later establishment of a constitutional republic in the United States.
- **Rule of Law:** A list of grievances against the monarch of England, King George III was included within the Declaration. Although not explicitly stated, this inclusion implies that no ruler should live above the law and that those in government must be subject to the same laws and legal proceedings as the citizenry. A constitutional republic cannot function appropriately in situations where elected officials are seen as living above the law. Consequently, the rule of law represents an essential component of all constitutional republics, including that of the United States.

40

These principles helped to shape the system of governance still in effect in the United States today and represent key elements of constitutional republics worldwide.

PRINCIPLES THAT ALLOWED FOR THE GROWTH OF CIVIL RIGHTS IN THE US

Throughout the course of United States history, civil rights have been expanded so that all groups experience equal protection under the law. This expansion has been driven largely by the principle of **equality**, or the belief that all people—regardless of gender, race, or any other category—are created equally and are deserving of equal treatment. This notion was initially introduced in the United States with the drafting of the Declaration of Independence (1776). The Declaration specifically states that "All Men are created equal" and that all are endowed with certain rights that are unalienable. Although this principle was applied to only a limited number of people early on in American history, these rights were expanded over time through a variety of amendments to the Constitution and Supreme Court rulings to apply to the American populace as a whole. Today, the legacy of the Declaration of Independence has led to a system in which all US citizens' rights are valued and protected.

The Constitution of Massachusetts

CHARACTERISTICS OF THE CONSTITUTION OF MASSACHUSETTS

Primarily written by John Adams—a Founding Father who championed the independence movement in the American colonies and who would later go on to serve as the second President of the United States—the **Constitution of Massachusetts** was ratified on June 15, 1780. Recognized as the oldest written constitution still in effect today, the document established a system of state governance in Massachusetts that greatly influenced the United States Constitution (1787). Many important Enlightenment (1685–1815) ideals are engrained in the Constitution of Massachusetts, including the separation of governmental power into three branches, popular sovereignty, and a focus on the rights of the individual. The document begins with the Declaration of Rights, which details the protection of inalienable rights such as freedom of speech and religion. Ultimately, many of the key elements of the Constitution of Massachusetts were later incorporated into the United States Constitution and continue to serve as the basis for constitutional republics around the world.

INFLUENCE OF THE CONSTITUTION OF MASSACHUSETTS ON THE DEVELOPMENT OF THE US AS A CONSTITUTIONAL REPUBLIC

The Constitution of Massachusetts (1780) serves as the oldest known written constitution still in use today. Many elements of the Constitution of Massachusetts were adopted into the United States Constitution (1787), with the earlier document seen as a model of sorts for the governing structure of the US government.

- **Popular Sovereignty:** The Constitution of Massachusetts states that the people of Massachusetts have the right to govern themselves and that the people serve as the source of governmental power. Additionally, if the government infringes upon the rights of the people, the people have the right to alter or overthrow the government to ensure their needs are met.
- **Separation of Powers:** The Constitution of Massachusetts established a system of governance in which power was divided between three separate branches: a powerful Executive Branch, an independent Judicial Branch, and a Legislative Branch.
- **Bill of Rights:** A Declaration of Rights is included within the Constitution of Massachusetts that explicitly details the rights of the citizens of Massachusetts.

41

Ultimately, these three provisions significantly influenced the development of the United States Constitution and the ensuing system of US government.

The Articles of Confederation

The **Articles of Confederation** was ratified in 1781 and served as the first constitution or written framework of the American states. Written primarily by John Dickinson (1732–1808), a delegate to the Second Continental Congress from Delaware, the document served as a guideline for the operation of American government during the Revolutionary War (1775–1783) as well as in the initial years of independence from the British Crown. The Articles outlined the powers and responsibilities of the central and state governments. State governments were granted a disproportionate amount of power compared to the relatively weak central government. For example, the central government, or Congress, had the ability to declare war and conduct diplomatic relations but not the ability to levy taxes or raise an army to help exercise these powers. The colonists feared a strong central authority that held power similar to that wielded by the King of England. Additionally, the colonies failed to recognize themselves as a unified state, hence the creation of a **confederacy**, or set of states loosely aligned for a few shared interests. Ultimately, the Articles of Confederation proved largely ineffective. The economy struggled profusely under the Articles, and Congress was unable to effectively mediate state disputes or lead a unified nation. The Founding Fathers determined that a new system of governance with a stronger central authority must be established, leading to the Constitutional Convention in 1787 and the creation of the United States Constitution that same year.

INTELLECTUAL INFLUENCES THAT SHAPED THE DEVELOPMENT OF THE ARTICLES OF CONFEDERATION

Ratified in 1781, the Articles of Confederation served as the first constitution of the United States of America. The document created a loose confederation of states that was unified for the purpose of defense and mutual cooperation in certain areas. The Articles established a **unicameral**, or one-house, legislature that served as the central government and that held limited powers, such as waging war and maintaining diplomatic relations with foreign governments. The central government lacked the authority to tax, raise an army, or enforce laws effectively; all of which contributed to its weaknesses. A number of intellectual theories and philosophies shaped the development of the Articles of Confederation.

- **Social Contract Theory:** John Locke and other Enlightenment (1685–1815) thinkers theorized that citizens of a state enter into a social contract, in which they give up certain rights in exchange for protection from the government. Consequently, the people provide consent to be governed. This concept is engrained in several places in the Articles, as well as the states' agreement to voluntarily relinquish a degree of power to the central government in exchange for mutual protection.
- **Limited Government:** The notion that government should be limited in its scope to prevent the development of tyrannical rule weighed heavily on the authors of the Articles of Confederation. The Founding Fathers feared that creating a strong central government with broad scope and powers could allow a regime similar to that of the British monarchy to emerge. Consequently, the Founders chose to concentrate power in the hands of the state government while creating a weak central authority that was unable to act unilaterally.

- **Self-Governance:** Emerging from a history of British rule, the Founding Fathers felt compelled to establish a system of self-governance in which governmental decisions were made by the American people without the encroachment of outside influences. The authors of the Articles looked at earlier state constitutions as well as the **Mayflower Compact (1620)**, which laid out the Pilgrims' system of self-governance in the New World.

Although the Articles of Confederation was relatively short-lived, it served as an important stepping stone in the US government's development.

PRINCIPLES THAT LED TO THE DEVELOPMENT OF THE US AS A CONSTITUTIONAL REPUBLIC

The Articles of Confederation (1781) served as the first constitution of the United States of America. Although the Articles ultimately proved ineffective and led to the development of a weak central government, many of the principles included in the document laid the groundwork for the constitutional republic still in existence in the United States today. The Articles introduced a system of **Federalism**, where power was shared between two levels of government: the central government, comprised of a unicameral legislature, and the state governments. Although the power dynamics are different in modern US government, power is still divided between the federal and state governments. Similarly, **state sovereignty** represented a key component of the Articles of Confederation that is still in place today. Under the Articles, states held significant power at the expense of a weak central government. In the country's current constitutional republic, states retain sovereignty in many areas, but they ultimately ceded significant power to the federal government in the Constitution's creation of dual sovereignty. The Articles also incorporated the notion of **limited government**, in which the power of the state is limited to prevent tyranny. The Founders feared that a strong central authority may allow for unchecked power, similar to that of the King of England; this fear contributed to the development of a weak central government. Although the federal government gained significant powers and responsibilities under the US Constitution (1787), its power is still limited to prevent an ultimate abuse of power. These principles, while altered to a degree under the Constitution, led to the modern constitutional republic that exists in the United States today.

STRENGTHS AND WEAKNESSES

The Articles of Confederation represented the first constitution of the American states. The document, which was adopted by the Second Constitutional Congress in 1777 and ratified by the states in 1781, developed a weak central government and concentrated most governmental power in the hands of the states. Although the Articles did have several strengths—including the fact that the document unified the states into one cohesive unit, allowed for the conduction of diplomacy with foreign states, and preserved the sovereignty of the states—it ultimately proved to be an ineffective system of governance. The central government, which comprised the **Confederation Congress** where each state had one vote regardless of population, did not have the authority to raise an army or to levy taxes so that any armed forces could be effectively funded. Instead, the central government relied on the states to provide militias when a need for military arose, but states could easily ignore Congress's requests for militias with no repercussions. Additionally, no true central authority in the form of an executive branch to enforce legislation or a judiciary branch to resolve disputes existed. This resulted in a largely ineffective government that was unable to accomplish traditional government duties. Finally, unanimous agreement among the states was required before any amendments could be made to the Articles. This resulted in an inability to make the changes necessary to establish a fully functioning and effective system of governance. These weaknesses led to calls from members of Congress to revise the Articles of Confederation at the Constitutional Convention of 1787.

REFLECTION OF IDEAS PRESENTED IN THE DECLARATION OF INDEPENDENCE

The Articles of Confederation, which was adopted in 1777 and ratified in 1781, served as the first constitution of the United States. Many of the ideals presented in the **Declaration of Independence** (1776) were also present in the Articles of Confederation. For example, both documents focused on the importance of self-governance and limiting the power of the government to prevent tyrannical rule. Beyond these similarities, the influence of the Articles of Confederation on the development of the **United States Constitution** (1787) was even greater. The Articles of Confederation established a loose confederation of states in which the central government was provided with very limited powers. This prevented the government from carrying out tasks that were essential to both governmental operations and the American people as a whole. When drafting the Constitution, the Founding Fathers understood that although it was important to maintain a limited government that focused on self-governance and state sovereignty to a degree, the power of the central government must be greatly expanded. In order to ensure that the power of the central or federal government did not become tyrannical, the Founders incorporated concepts such as the separation of powers, checks and balances, and federalism into the Constitution.

The Northwest Ordinances

OVERVIEW

The Northwest Ordinances were three laws that detailed the expansion of the United States of America into the Northwest Territory, or any land north of the Ohio River, west of the Appalachian Mountains, and east of the Mississippi River.

- **Northwest Ordinance of 1784:** Thomas Jefferson (1743–1826) outlined a plan to divide the Northwest Territory into individual districts and eventual states. This ordinance also detailed the way by which territories should become states upon reaching a certain population (20,000 inhabitants), and it allowed for a republican form of government, in which power rests with the people who elect officials to govern on their behalf.
- **Northwest Ordinance of 1785:** This ordinance provided for a system by which land in the Northwest Territory should be surveyed and sold. Land was divided into townships, which were then divided up using grids for settlement purposes.
- **Northwest Ordinance of 1787:** Often recognized as the most influential, the Ordinance of 1787 provided for a system of governance and ultimate statehood in each territory. It also guaranteed the protection of important rights, such as due process and religious freedom, for settlers. Slavery was also banned in the Northwest Territory through this ordinance, and a protocol was established for interactions with Native Americans.

Ultimately, these ordinances allowed for a structured expansion of the United States.

INTELLECTUAL INFLUENCES ON THE NORTHWEST ORDINANCES

The Northwest Ordinances (1784–1787), a series of three laws that guided the expansion of the United States into the Northwest Territory, were influenced by a variety of intellectual principles and philosophies.

- **Enlightenment Values:** The Enlightenment (1685–1815) focused on the expansion of natural rights for all men, including property ownership and a number of other personal freedoms. Furthermore, the concept of social contract—in which the government governs with the consent of the people, who in turn provide the government with its authority—also serves as an important aspect of Enlightenment thought. The Northwest Ordinances provided an avenue for individuals residing in the Northwest Territory to purchase land. Furthermore, The Northwest Ordinance of 1787 guaranteed many further protections, such as religious freedom and due process.
- **Republican Principles:** The Northwest Ordinances focused on republican principles such as property rights, self-governance, and educational opportunities. For example, the Ordinances divided available land into townships. The land was then allotted in a way that reserved a section of each township for a public school to be built, demonstrating the importance of education.
- **Abolitionism:** Although the US Constitution initially protected the institution of slavery, many such provisions were included only to ensure ratification by the southern states. Conversely, the Northwest Ordinances banned the practice of slavery throughout the Northwest Territory. This further highlighted Enlightenment principles, such as equality and the protection of individual rights regardless of social standing.

The Northwest Ordinances relied heavily on early political thought and worked to expand Enlightenment ideals and civil liberties beyond the traditional borders of the American states.

Federalist Papers

The **Federalist Papers** were a collection of 85 essays drafted between 1787 and 1788 by Alexander Hamilton (1755–1804), John Jay (1745–1829), and James Madison (1751–1836) under the name Publius. They were written to elicit support for the ratification of the United States Constitution (1787). The essays detailed the need for a strong central government to address the inherent weaknesses of the Articles of Confederation (1777), and they focused on topics such as the separation of powers and the system of checks and balances established by the US Constitution. The Federalist Papers also argued against claims made by the **Anti-Federalists**, a group of delegates to the Constitutional Convention who feared the establishment of a strong central government. The Federalist Papers resulted in increased public support and eventual ratification of the United States Constitution by the states.

KEY TAKEAWAYS OF FEDERALIST PAPERS NUMBERS 10, 14, 31, 39, AND 51

The Federalist Papers were written between 1787 and 1788 to garner support for the ratification of the United States Constitution (1787).

- **Federalist No. 10** was written by James Madison (1751–1836) to discuss the dangers associated with **factions**, or small groups of individuals within a government that may operate in a way that is harmful to the public good. Madison argued that only a large republican government, such as the one proposed in the Constitution, can negate the dangers associated with factions through the dispersal of power, which will prevent any singular faction from becoming too powerful. A pure democracy is not equipped for this task.
- **Federalist No. 14**, also written by James Madison, addressed claims by the Anti-Federalists that a republic would be an ineffective form of governance for a large state. Madison stated that large republics are more stable and more effective at overcoming the danger of factions than smaller ones. Furthermore, Madison argued that the system of **checks and balances**, as well as the representative nature of the government, would ensure that the government was reactive and accountable to the needs of the people.
- **Federalist No. 31** was written by Alexander Hamilton (1755–1804) to argue that a strong federal government was necessary to maintain a stable system of government in which all citizens' rights were protected. Hamilton claimed that a strong central government was needed to maintain unity across the states and to allow for the effective enforcement of laws.
- **Federalist No. 39** was written by James Madison in response to claims by Anti-Federalists that the Constitution was not republican or federal. Madison asserted that the new government was republican, in that its power was derived from the people and administered by those whom they had elected. He also detailed the federal and national nature of the government, responding to claims that the government would be national and not federal.
- **Federalist No. 51** was also written by James Madison, who explained the importance of the separation of powers and system of checks and balances to protect American freedoms. Madison argued that each branch must have enough power to resist influence by the other branches to ensure that no one branch could become dominant. Madison also explained the need for a federal system of government, in which power was divided between federal and state governments to safeguard against tyrannical rule and protect the rights of the people.

Together these documents led to increased public support for the Constitution and, ultimately, to its ratification in 1787.

PRINCIPLES IN THE FEDERALIST PAPERS THAT SHAPED THE DEVELOPMENT OF THE US

The Federalist Papers were written by Alexander Hamilton (1755–1804), John Jay (1745–1829), and James Madison (1751–1836) between 1787 and 1788 to increase public support for the ratification of the United States Constitution (1787). Many of the ideals mentioned within the Federalist Papers were a confirmation or argument for the Constitution itself. Consequently, there exists a strong connection between the Federalist Papers and the development of a constitutional republic in the United States of America.

- **Popular Sovereignty**, the notion that the government is created by the people and is subject to their will, is a vital component of constitutional republics. In Federalist No. 1, James Madison explained that the system of government proposed by the Constitution reflects the will of the people and ensures that individual liberties are protected.
- **Checks and Balances**, the ability of each branch of government to "check" another branch, effectively limiting its power, represents a characteristic of a constitutional republic in the United States. Federalist No. 51, written by Madison, highlights the importance of incorporating checks and balances to prevent abuses of power and to maintain liberty for all.
- **Separation of Powers** serves as another important principle associated with constitutional republics that was reiterated in the Federalist Papers. Federalist No. 51 and Federalist No. 47, both written by Madison, explain the importance of dividing power between the three branches of government to safeguard against tyranny.
- **The Rule of Law**, or the philosophy that government officials must be subject to the same laws as everyday citizens, stands out as a key characteristic of the American constitutional republic. In Federalist No. 78, Alexander Hamilton outlined the importance of the federal courts in serving as an intermediary between the legislature and the people. This ensures that Congress acts only within the powers granted by the Constitution.
- **Federalism**, or the division of power between federal and state governments, contributed significantly to the current model of government in the United States. Federalist No. 39, written by Madison, explains how the new system of governance will be a federal model.

Ultimately, these principles evident throughout the Federalist Papers shaped the development of a constitutional republic in the United States.

ARGUMENTS PRESENTED BY THE FEDERALISTS IN FAVOR OF THE RATIFICATION OF THE US CONSTITUTION

Many of the arguments surrounding the ratification of the United States Constitution (1787) centered around the balance of power between federal and state governments. The Federalists argued that in order to be effective, the federal government required additional strength bolstered by a powerful legislature, independent judiciary, and the establishment of a true executive branch. Although the Federalists acknowledged that the Constitution brought about a significant increase of power at the national level, they argued that this power would be tempered by important elements, such as the separation of power between the three branches of government, checks and balances to control power between the branches, and the division of power between the federal and state governments. Given the flaws of the Articles of Confederation (1777), the first constitution of the United States, those in support of the US Constitution felt that a strong central government was the only solution to rectifying the weakness of the then-current system of government. Furthermore, the Federalists asserted that the aforementioned limitations ensured that the government would never infringe on the rights of the people and that adding these limitations to the Constitution would create a governing doctrine that would withstand the test of time.

Founding Documents

United States Constitution

INFLUENCE OF THE ENLIGHTENMENT ON THE DRAFTING OF THE US CONSTITUTION

The United States Constitution, written in 1787 primarily by James Madison (1751–1836), Alexander Hamilton (1755–1804), John Jay (1745–1829), and ratified by the states in 1788 was heavily influenced by Enlightenment ideals. **The Enlightenment** was an intellectual movement during the 17th and 18th centuries that focused on individual rights, logic, and reason as a basis for governmental and societal change. The theories of John Locke (1632–1704), the Baron de Montesquieu (1689–1755), and Jean-Jacques Rousseau (1712–1778) are evident throughout the Constitution and are considered some of the primary influences on its creation. Locke theorized that one of the primary purposes of government was to protect the natural rights of man: life, liberty, and property. Furthermore, Locke asserted that man enters into a **social contract** with the government through which the government must protect these rights. A government that fails to carry out this task must be replaced. The social contract and protection of individual rights in general tie directly to the Constitution's focus on popular sovereignty, or the notion that governmental power is created by and ultimately rests with the people. Additionally, Montesquieu detailed the importance of a **separation of powers** between three branches of government: an Executive, Legislative, and Judicial Branch, each with its own powers and responsibilities. The separation of powers between three such branches is a hallmark of the American governmental system that is explicitly described in the Constitution. Finally, Rousseau also argued the importance of popular sovereignty and the **general will** of the people to an effective governmental system. According to Rousseau, the general will, or the desires of the people in their capacity as citizens, must be carried out through their right to legislate. The Constitution outlines the representative nature of the government and the way by which the people can engage in the legislative process. Ultimately, these Enlightenment ideas and others helped to shape the Constitution and the US governmental system in general.

INTELLECTUAL INFLUENCES OF THE US CONSTITUTION

The United States Constitution was drafted in 1787 in hopes of developing an effective system of governance that would withstand the test of time. Although the new system of government would prove to be innovative, it was largely based on earlier pre-established philosophies.

- **Republicanism:** Republicanism can be understood as a system of government that focuses on the rule of law, representative governance, and civic responsibility. The classical republics of Greece and Rome, and their governmental philosophies, greatly informed the development of the US Constitution. The Founding Fathers were influenced significantly by early democratic systems utilized in both Ancient Rome and Greece. These concepts are engrained throughout the Constitution, as evidenced by its establishment of a representative government that is limited in scope.
- **Enlightenment Principles:** Enlightenment principles like John Locke's focus on social contract theory and protection of individual rights and de Montesquieu's principle of the separation of powers proved instrumental to the development of the Constitution. These philosophies led to the safeguarding of essential civil liberties throughout the Constitution and Bill of Rights, as well as the division of power between three branches of government: the Legislative, Executive, and Judicial Branches.

48

- **English Traditions:** The framers of the Constitution were also influenced by traditional English legal doctrine. Documents such as the **Magna Carta** (1215), which limited the power of the British King and provided rights to the British nobility, and the **English Bill of Rights** (1689), which further limited the power of the King and provided additional freedoms to the British people, also served as an important influence for the structure, layout, and protections included in the US Constitution.

Ultimately, the US Constitution was borrowed from earlier political thought to establish a system of government that would be emulated by countries around the globe.

IDEALS INCLUDED IN THE CONSTITUTION THAT SHAPED THE DEVELOPMENT OF THE US

The United States is known as a **constitutional republic**, meaning that although the government is established and granted power by the people themselves, those same people elect officials to make governmental decisions on their behalf. In this type of government, the actions and powers of the government are detailed and limited by a **constitution**, a formal written document describing the layout of the government and the rules and regulations for those in power. In the United States, several key ideals present in the **US Constitution** (1787) serve as essential elements that shaped the development of a constitutional republic in America. **Republicanism** represents the first important principle, as it states that the people hold the power and elect officials to serve on their behalf. **Limited government** and **popular sovereignty** also serve as important principles engrained in the US system of governance, as they pertain to the source of and limitations on state power. The concept of limited government mandates that no governmental official lives above the law, while popular sovereignty establishes the American people as the source of governmental power. The **separation of powers** and **federalism** are two additional principles of governance that detail the structure of the US government. Separation of powers can be understood as the division of power between three branches of power: the Executive, Legislative, and Judicial Branches, while federalism characterizes the division of power between the federal and state levels of government. Together these characteristics establish a constitutional republic that serves the will of the people, while allowing for less direct involvement in daily governmental decisions.

HOW THE CONSTITUTION CONTRIBUTED TO THE EXPANSION OF CIVIL LIBERTIES OVER TIME

The United States Constitution (1787) laid the foundation for the expansion of civil liberties in the United States of America through its protection of fundamental rights. Although the Constitution did not originally include a bill of rights that specifically outlined the protections granted to the American citizenry, the official Bill of Rights was ultimately proposed and ratified in 1791. The Bill of Rights details essential freedoms, such as freedom of religion and freedom of speech, and it protects against governmental overreach, including unreasonable search and seizure. Upon the initial adoption of the Constitution, these protections only extended to certain individuals, and various minority groups were excluded. As time progressed, additional amendments such as the **Thirteenth Amendment**, which banned slavery, and the **Fourteenth Amendment**, which guaranteed equal protection under the law, were passed to promote a greater degree of equity and overall expansion of civil rights.

ARGUMENTS PRESENTED IN FAVOR OF THE RATIFICATION OF THE US CONSTITUTION

Many of the arguments surrounding the ratification of the United States Constitution (1787) centered around the balance of power between federal and state governments. Two main camps emerged in the lead-up to the ratification of the Constitution: **The Federalists**, who supported the ratification of the Constitution, and the **Anti-Federalists**, who disagreed with the system of government established by the Constitution due to a fear of a strong centralized authority. The Federalists argued that in order to be effective, the federal government required additional strength

49

bolstered by a powerful legislature, an independent judiciary, and the establishment of a true executive branch. Although the Federalists acknowledged that the Constitution brought about a significant increase of power at the national level, they argued that this power would be tempered by important elements such as the separation of power between the three branches of government, checks and balances to control power between the branches, and the ideal of federalism: the division of power between the federal and state governments. Given the flaws of the Articles of Confederation (1777), the first constitution of the United States, those in support of the US Constitution felt that a strong central government was the only solution to rectify the weakness of their current system of government. Furthermore, the Federalists asserted that the aforementioned limitations ensured that the government would never infringe on the rights of the people, and that these limitations would create a governing doctrine that would withstand the test of time.

Bill of Rights (1791)

INTELLECTUAL INFLUENCES THAT SHAPED THE DEVELOPMENT OF THE BILL OF RIGHTS

Comprising the first 10 amendments to the United States Constitution (1787), the **Bill of Rights (1791)** guarantees the protection of a number of essential freedoms to the American people. Important civil liberties, such as the freedoms of press, assembly, and religion, are explicitly detailed to ensure that the government does not infringe on the basic rights of the citizens. The Bill of Rights was influenced by a number of philosophies and principles that led to its ultimate creation.

- **Natural Rights Theory:** The belief that individuals possess certain inalienable rights by virtue of their position as human beings contributed greatly to the development of the Bill of Rights. This theory, championed by Enlightenment (1685–1815) thinkers, served as the basis for the Bill of Rights as a modification to the Constitution that details the rights of the American people.
- **Social Contract Theory:** Enlightenment thinkers such as John Locke, Jean-Jacques Rousseau, and Thomas Hobbes promoted the theory that governments rule with the consent of the governed and must protect personal freedoms in exchange. The Bill of Rights explicitly lists personal freedoms that must be protected by the government, with very limited exceptions.
- **English Common Law:** Documents such as the **Magna Carta (1215)**, which limited the power of the King, and the **English Bill of Rights (1689)**, which explicitly detailed the freedoms of the citizens, both contributed greatly to the Bill of Rights. Many of the Founding Fathers feared that the strong central government could infringe upon the rights of the citizens, and they felt strongly that the people's rights needed to be specifically delineated. Consequently, they looked to the governing documents introduced earlier in England.

Ultimately, these philosophies and others led to the addition of the Bill of Rights to the US Constitution.

PRINCIPLES THAT CONTRIBUTED TO THE EXPANSION OF CIVIL RIGHTS IN THE US

Comprising the first 10 amendments to the United States Constitution, the **Bill of Rights** (1791) outlines the specific freedoms that are guaranteed to the American people. Although initially narrow in scope, these rights were eventually expanded so that the individual freedoms of minority groups were also protected. Supreme Court rulings, legislative actions, and the ratification of the **Fourteenth Amendment** contributed to this expansion. For example, the landmark case *Miranda v Arizona* **(1966)** expanded the protections of the **Fifth Amendment** to require arresting officers to recite an individual's "**Miranda Rights**" when taking that individual into police custody. Additionally, with the passing of legislation such as the **Voting Rights Act of 1965** and the **Civil Rights Act of 1964**, voting rights were further protected for all US citizens. Following the adoption of the Bill of Rights, the amendments included applied only to the actions of the federal government; however, in 1868 the Fourteenth Amendment required that each amendment also extended to the states through a concept known as **incorporation**. This allowed the federal government to ensure that states were not engaging in discriminatory practices. The Bill of Rights provided a legal framework that, through a variety of rulings by the Supreme Court and later amendments, allowed for the expansion of civil rights for all citizens of the United States.

PRINCIPLES THAT SHAPED THE DEVELOPMENT OF THE US AS A CONSTITUTIONAL REPUBLIC

Adopted in 1791, the **Bill of Rights** helped shape the US as a constitutional republic by increasing protection of individual freedoms, putting more limitations on the government's power, and adding structure to the government. The first 10 amendments sought to ensure the protection of certain rights that the Founding Fathers saw as inalienable, including the freedoms of religion, speech, and assembly. These protections continue to serve as an important foundation for the US governmental system. Additionally, the Bill of Rights outlined a number of restrictions on governmental authority; it introduced procedures such as due process that must be followed while adjudicating an accused. Furthermore, the Bill of Rights, and specifically the **Tenth Amendment**, outlined the concept of **Federalism**, which it put into action by reserving powers not explicitly delegated to the federal government for the states. Federalism ensured that power was shared between the federal and state governments, and it promoted state sovereignty, a point of contention in the lead-up to the ratification of the US Constitution (1787). The Bill of Rights contributed greatly to the current constitutional republic in the United States.

ROLE IN THE RATIFICATION PROCESS OF THE US CONSTITUTION

In the lead-up to the ratification of the US Constitution in 1787, two general groups emerged: **Federalists** and **Anti-Federalists**. The Federalists argued that although the proposed system of government did result in a strong central government, this was necessary to establish an effective system of governance. They asserted that the various checks on power and the general governmental structure would protect against a tyrannical regime. Conversely, the Anti-Federalists decreed that the Constitution would result in a strong and tyrannical regime that infringed on the sovereignty of the states. They expressed concern that a bill of rights protecting the individual freedoms of citizens was not included, further augmenting the risk of a strong central government. As a result of the Anti-Federalists' concerns and in order to increase the likelihood of state ratification of the Constitution, especially in key states such as New York and Virginia where greater resistance existed, the Federalists promised to add a bill of rights after the official adoption of the Constitution. These promises ultimately led to the ratification of the Constitution as well as the safeguarding of individual freedoms for citizens through the addition of the Bill of Rights.

Founding Documents

Additional Founding Documents

SIGNIFICANCE OF THE MAGNA CARTA

Signed in 1215, the **Magna Carta** sought to limit the power of the King John of England as well as to provide certain protections to the English nobility. The Magna Carta introduced the notion of limited government as well as the rule of law to ensure that no one, not even the monarch himself, was above the law. These core concepts of the Magna Carta laid the foundation for the United States Constitution (1787). The Magna Carta protected English nobility against unfair treatment by the King, such as unjust imprisonments, and it guaranteed fair trials. The **Sixth Amendment** of the US Constitution guarantees citizens a fair trial and details a number of rights promised to the accused. Furthermore, the **Fifth Amendment** ensures the right to due process, or the notion that one cannot be deprived of liberty without governmental abidance to pre-established procedures and norms. Although some differences undoubtedly exist in regard to the scope and limitations of the Magna Carta in accordance with those of the US Constitution, clear connections exist between the two documents.

SIGNIFICANCE OF THE MAYFLOWER COMPACT

The Mayflower Compact was signed by the Pilgrims in 1620 on their voyage across the Atlantic Ocean aboard the Mayflower. The Pilgrims understood the need to develop a civil body politic, or temporary government, to guide not only the establishment of a system of government in the colonies but also interactions amongst the settlers. Consequently, the Pilgrims signed off on the Mayflower Compact, in which they agreed to enter into a social contract where authority was vested in the civil body politic, which in turn was based on the consent of the governed. The Mayflower Compact had a major impact on later iterations of American government.

- **Rule of Law:** The Mayflower Compact outlined the importance of establishing laws agreed to by the people to which all residents were bound. The United States government today is based in part on the notion that all citizens are subject to the same laws established by the democratically elected Congress regardless of their position in the government.
- **Self-Governance:** The Pilgrims were accustomed to rule by the British Monarchy, who saw their power as derived from God. The Mayflower Compact established a system based on self-governance in which the people held the power and were responsible for governing themselves.

Ultimately, the Mayflower Compact served as a precursor for the drafting and establishment of the Declaration of Independence (1776) and the United States Constitution (1787).

INFLUENCE OF THE ENGLISH BILL OF RIGHTS

The English Bill of Rights (1689) significantly influenced the development of the US governmental system through its establishment of principles such as limited government and the rule of law, as well as through its focus on the protection of individual rights. The power of the monarchy was limited through restrictions on the King's ability to override laws, maintain a standing army, or raise taxes without the explicit consent of the British Parliament. The Founding Fathers, who were familiar by virtue of their heritage with the legal traditions of England, relied heavily on the English Bill of Rights when drafting both the US Constitution (1787) and the Bill of Rights (1789). The US Constitution focuses heavily on limiting the power of government and incorporates the separation of powers and a system of checks and balances to prevent tyrannical rules, while the US Bill of Rights ensures that individual rights are explicitly protected. Ultimately, the English Bill of Rights helped to shape the core values of US governmental philosophy and led to not only the

establishment of the Constitution and Bill of Rights, but the current system of government in general.

INFLUENCE OF COMMON SENSE

Common Sense, a pamphlet written by Thomas Paine (1737–1809) in 1776 to advocate for independence from England, played a significant role in the establishment of self-governance in America. Paine argued that the only way to escape the oppressive policies of the British Crown was to seek independence from England and establish a democratic republic in the American colonies. In 1776, discontent regarding British treatment of the colonists—especially the fact that England was levying heavy taxes on the colonies without offering representation in British Parliament—was widespread throughout the American colonies. Paine argued that government should only be established with consent of the governed, a concept which laid the foundation for governance in the United States. Furthermore, Paine asserted that the colonies had the means, population, and overall right to govern themselves, which built confidence in the colonists that they could successfully establish and ultimately manage the operations of a sovereign state. *Common Sense* helped to unify the colonists and shift public opinion in support of independence from the British monarchy. The concepts of liberty, representative government, and equality became central to the development of an independent American state.

INFLUENCE OF THE VIRGINIA DECLARATION OF RIGHTS

The Virginia Declaration of Rights was written in 1776 by George Mason (1725–1792) to outline the rights of the citizens of Virginia following their decision to break free from the British empire. The declaration was to coincide with a written constitution aimed to frame a new system of governance in the state of Virginia. Mason drafted a 10-paragraph declaration that detailed many protections, such as protection from self-incrimination and cruel and unusual punishment, as well as the right to a speedy and fair trial. The Virginia Declaration of Rights served as an important influence for the **United States Bill of Rights** (1789), the first 10 amendments to the US Constitution which outlined many important civil liberties and protections. James Madison (1751–1836), the primary author of the Bill of Rights, adopted many of the safeguards included in the Virginia Declaration of Rights; however, Madison expanded on the protections included in the earlier framework by incorporating further rights such as the freedom of speech and the ability to petition the government. Furthermore, Madison expanded on the ability of Americans to practice religion freely, replacing religious tolerance with true religious freedom. The Bill of Rights serves as an essential component of the American governmental system, one which was heavily influenced by the Virginia Declaration of Rights.

CONTRIBUTION OF THE ANTI-FEDERALIST PAPERS

The Anti-Federalist Papers, a series of essays written by individuals that opposed the ratification of the United State Constitution (1787), stated that the system of government proposed by the Constitution created a central government that was too strong and threatened the civil liberties of the American people. The Anti-Federalists asserted that the only way to effectively deter the establishment of a tyrannical regime was to incorporate a bill of rights into the Constitution that specifically delineated the rights of the American people. The most significant Anti-Federalist papers were written under the pseudonym Brutus, with the paper known as Brutus No. 1 standing out as the most influential to the Anti-Federalists' cause. Most likely drafted by New York judge Robert Yates (1738–1801), Brutus No. 1 detailed the purported dangers of a strong central government. Of particular concern was the **Necessary and Proper Clause** of the Constitution, which allowed Congress to carry out duties seen as necessary to those explicitly listed in the Constitution, as well as the **Supremacy Clause**, which impeded on state sovereignty. Furthermore, Brutus No. 1 highlighted concerns regarding the establishment of a republic which may be unable

Founding Documents

53

to meet the needs of a diverse populace. Brutus No. 1 also reiterated the concerns of the Anti-Federalists regarding a lack of a bill of rights to protect the rights of the American people against a large and powerful government. Ultimately, Brutus No. 1, and the Anti-Federalist Papers in general, led to widespread discussion regarding the ratification of the Constitution. The Federalists were forced to promise the addition of a bill of rights in exchange for the ultimate ratification of the Constitution. The concerns of the Anti-Federalist led to the establishment of a government that was more focused on the protection of individual rights, as well as on limiting the power of the government.

Landmark Supreme Court Cases, Legislation, and Executive Actions

Landmark Cases

IMPORTANCE OF LANDMARK SUPREME COURT CASES

Landmark Supreme Court cases are those cases decided by the Supreme Court that carry significant implications for US society or governmental operations. Often, landmark cases seek to clarify the true meaning of the US Constitution (1787) as applied to controversial or significant societal issues. By virtue of the Constitution, the Judicial Branch, particularly the Supreme Court, is granted the right to interpret the meaning of the Constitution; this legal interpretation is a necessity given the broad nature of the document. The Founding Fathers intended the Supreme Court to serve as a "check" on both the Legislative and Executive Branches to prevent abuses of power and protect the rights of the people. Landmark cases heard and ruled on by the Supreme Court often deal with issues pertaining to civil rights and the power of the government. Such cases establish **legal precedence**, or a model on which future courts can base their decisions when presented with similar issues. Consequently, landmark cases typically impact not only the justice system but society at large. In general, landmark cases have helped to expand minority rights, limit governmental overreach, and ensure that governmental decisions reflect the societal changes that have occurred since the drafting of the Constitution.

MARBURY V MADISON

Marbury v Madison was an 1803 Supreme Court case that established a standard for the constitutional power of the Supreme Court to carry out **judicial review of federal statutes**. The Supreme Court decided that it had the power to invalidate a statute that it found to be in violation of the Constitution. The case established the Judicial Branch as an equal counterpart to the other two branches of the United States federal government. Specifically, *Marbury v Madison* was the inaugural case during which the United States Supreme Court used the power of judicial review.

> **Review Video: Marbury v Madison**
> Visit mometrix.com/academy and enter code: 573964

MCCULLOCH V MARYLAND

McCulloch v Maryland was a landmark case that established the supremacy of the federal government over state governments and clarified the implied powers of the United States Congress. The case originated when the State of Maryland attempted to tax the Second Bank of the United States, claiming that the Constitution of the United States did not grant Congress the power to establish a national bank. When a bank official, James McCulloch, refused to pay the tax, the issue was brought before the Supreme Court. In the majority opinion and reflecting a unanimous decision by the Court, Chief Justice of the Supreme Court **John Marshall** (1755–1835) held that as a result of the **Necessary and Proper Clause**, a clause of the Constitution that grants Congress the ability to pass laws seen as necessary in carrying out their enumerated powers, Congress did in fact possess the power to establish a national bank. Furthermore, the Court held that although state governments bear the power to tax, that power does not extend to taxing the federal government; taxing the federal government would violate the **Supremacy Clause** of the Constitution, a provision which establishes federal law and the Constitution in general as the supreme law of the land that must take precedence over state laws. Ultimately, *McCulloch v Maryland* solidified the power of the

federal government over that of the states and granted Congress considerable scope beyond the powers explicitly granted to the Legislative Branch in the Constitution.

DRED SCOTT V SANDFORD

Dred Scott v Sandford (1857) represents an important Supreme Court case that ultimately led to the denial of citizenship for African Americans and upheld slavery in the United States and its territories. Dred Scott, an enslaved man residing in Missouri, sued for his freedom based on his residency in a territory where slavery had been banned by the Missouri Compromise. In a 7–2 decision drafted by Chief Justice Roger Taney, the Supreme Court argued that African Americans held no right to citizenship and therefore lacked the right to sue in federal court. Furthermore, the Court ruled that Congress lacked the ability to ban slavery in US territories, rendering the Missouri Compromise (1820) unconstitutional. Finally, the Court argued that under the Fifth Amendment of the US Constitution (1787), enslaved individuals were considered as property, and that property rights were explicitly protected by the Constitution. This negated any claim to citizenship made by Scott. *Dred Scott v Sandford* ultimately led to increased tensions in the lead-up to the Civil War and expanded slavery's reach beyond the American South.

PLESSY V FERGUSON

Plessy v Ferguson was an 1896 Supreme Court case. The case resulted in the decision that **de jure racial segregation** in **public facilities** was legal in the United States and that states were permitted to restrict black people from using public facilities. The case originated when, in 1890, a mixed-race man named Homer Plessy decided to challenge a Louisiana law that segregated black and white people on trains by sitting in the white section of a train. Plessy was convicted of breaking the law in a Louisiana court, and the case was appealed to the US Supreme Court, where the Supreme Court upheld the Louisiana decision. The case established the legality of the doctrine of "separate but equal," thereby allowing racial segregation. The decision was later overturned by **Brown v the Board of Education of Topeka**.

SCHENCK V UNITED STATES

Schenck v United States (1919) played an important role in determining the limits of the freedom of speech guaranteed by the **First Amendment** of the United States Constitution (1787), ultimately establishing the **clear and present danger test** as a means of determining when the government can limit free speech. The case arose when Charles Schenck, a known socialist, began distributing leaflets encouraging others to resist the military draft, as he felt the draft represented a violation of people's rights. Schenck was arrested and convicted under the Espionage Act (1917) for alleged conspiracy to violate its provisions. Schenck appealed his conviction to the Supreme Court of the United States. In a unanimous decision drafted by Chief Justice Oliver Wendell Holmes Jr (1841–1935), the Court upheld the ruling of the lower court, arguing that the First Amendment does not protect speech that poses a clear and present danger of evoking harm. The ruling emphasized the point that some speech cannot be protected when it presents a risk to national security or public safety. Although future cases established greater understanding as to when and if speech should be limited, *Schenck v US* provided an important foundation for better understanding the scope of free speech.

KOREMATSU V UNITED STATES

During World War II, the US frequently denied civil liberties to Japanese Americans, forcing many to live in internment camps. In **Korematsu v US** (1944), the Supreme Court ruled that the internment camps were legal, but in **Ex parte Endo** (1944), the Court adjusted its decision to state that the US could only intern those whose disloyalty could be proven.

BROWN V BOARD OF EDUCATION OF TOPEKA

Brown v Board of Education of Topeka was a Supreme Court case that was decided in 1954. The case made it illegal for **racial segregation** to exist within **public education facilities**. This decision was based on the finding that "separate but equal" public educational facilities would not provide black and white students with the same standard of facilities. The case originated in 1951, when a lawsuit was filed by Topeka parents recruited by the NAACP against the Board of Education of the City of Topeka, Kansas in a US district court. The parents, one of whom was named Oliver Brown, wanted the Topeka Board of Education to eliminate racial segregation. The district court agreed that segregation had negative effects, but it did not force the schools to desegregate because it found that black and white school facilities in the district were generally equal in standards. The case was appealed to the Supreme Court, where the finding was that separate educational facilities are unequal.

MAPP V OHIO

The landmark Supreme Court case *Mapp v Ohio* (1961) established the application of the **exclusionary rule**—a legal principle that prevents evidence obtained through illegal searches and seizures from being used in court—to state as well as federal courts. The case began in 1957 when the home of Dollree Mapp was unlawfully searched by police without a warrant. The police entered the premises under the belief that Mapp was housing a fugitive; however, upon searching Mapp's home, they found a chest containing obscene photographs and arrested Mapp for possession of those photographs. Mapp argued that the unlawful search of her home violated her rights as protected by the **Fourth Amendment** of the United States Constitution (1787). The Court ruled in favor of Mapp, with the 6–3 majority arguing that evidence seized unlawfully was ineligible for use by state prosecutors in criminal cases. Ultimately, this decision extended the use of the exclusionary rule, which had historically been applied to federal cases through the use of the **Due Process Clause** of the **Fourteenth Amendment**. *Mapp v Ohio* also solidified the notion that the Constitution applies equally to both federal and state governments.

BAKER V CARR

Baker v Carr (1962) was a landmark Supreme Court case that determined the ability of federal courts to hear cases involving redistricting. Charles Baker, a resident of Tennessee, sued state officials, arguing that the system used to establish congressional districts was outdated and unfairly provided greater representation to individuals in rural areas at the expense of those residing in urban areas, despite significant population changes. Baker argued that the current distribution violated the **Equal Protection Clause** of the **Fourteenth Amendment**. Although Tennessee responded that redistricting was a political issue outside of the jurisdiction of the courts, in a 6–2 decision, the Supreme Court ruled that federal courts had the right to intervene in cases that pertained to the violation of constitutional rights. Although the Court did not require that new maps be drawn, this decision led to future rulings such as *Reynolds v Sims* (1964), which required congressional districts to include roughly equal population numbers. Ultimately, *Baker v Carr* led to fairer representation in both state and federal legislatures.

ENGEL V VITALE

Engel v Vitale (1962) solidified the principle of **separation of church and state** through its ruling that school-sponsored prayer in public schools was unconstitutional. In New York, a public school encouraged voluntary prayer to begin the school day. Steven Engel, along with a group of other parents from the school, argued that the practice violated the **Establishment Clause** of the **First Amendment**, which prevents the government from sanctioning or endorsing a specific religion. In turn, the state, represented by William Vitale, claimed that the practice was in line with the US

Landmark Supreme Court Cases, Legislation, and Executive Actions

57

Constitution (1787) given the optional, non-denominational nature of the prayer. In a 6–1 decision, the Court ruled in favor of Engel, stating that prayer in any form sanctioned by a public school was an example of involvement by the government in a religious matter. The Court held that the government must remain neutral in religious matters and that the practice carried out by the New York school could be construed as indirectly coercive. Ultimately, the case established an important precedent on the separation of church and state that continues to guide governmental operation on religious matters.

GIDEON V WAINWRIGHT

The landmark case **Gideon v Wainwright** (1963) established the guarantee to an attorney for individuals adjudicated in state courts. The State of Florida arrested Clarence Earl Gideon on the charge of felony breaking and entering. Gideon appeared in court without an attorney, citing a financial inability to pay the associated fees and requesting state-provided counsel. The State of Florida declined the request, as they only provided legal counsel to defendants facing capital murder charges. Consequently, Gideon represented himself in court, and he was found guilty of the charges against him. Gideon petitioned the Supreme Court to hear the case, arguing that his **Sixth Amendment** rights had been violated. The Court ruled in favor of Gideon in a unanimous decision, overturning an earlier precedent established by *Betts v Brady* (1942) which allowed for state denial of counsel in some situations. The Court argued that the right to counsel guaranteed by the Sixth Amendment applied to the states through the Fourteenth Amendment. As a result of this case, states must provide representation to defendants who are unable to afford legal fees, bringing about more equitable treatment in courts across the United States.

MIRANDA V ARIZONA

The landmark Supreme Court case **Miranda v Arizona** (1966) further developed the individual's protection from self-incrimination by requiring police officers to inform an offender of his or her rights under the **Fifth and Sixth Amendments** of the United States Constitution (1787). Ernesto Miranda was arrested in Arizona on charges of assault and kidnapping. Upon being questioned by the police, and without being informed of his rights, Miranda confessed to the crime. The state used his confession as evidence in court, and he was convicted and sentenced. The Supreme Court ruled in favor of Miranda in a 5–4 decision, writing that a suspect must be directly informed of his or her rights prior to custodial interrogation. As Miranda had not been informed of his rights prior to questioning, the confession was deemed inadmissible by the Court. The case ultimately led to the creation of **Miranda Rights**: essential rights that must be read to the offender prior to interrogation in police custody. Miranda Rights include the following and have become a part of a standardized procedure prior to police questioning in departments across the United States.

- The right to remain silent
- A statement that anything said can be used in court
- The right to an attorney
- A statement that if an individual cannot afford an attorney, one will be provided

TINKER V DES MOINES

Tinker v Des Moines (1969) was a landmark Supreme Court case that upheld the **First Amendment** rights of students while in school. During the Vietnam War, a group of students in Des Moines, Iowa, elected to wear black armbands to school in protest of the war. School administrators banned the armbands and suspended students who failed to comply with the ban. The family of John Tinker, one of the students suspended, chose to sue the school, arguing that the actions of the school violated the students' constitutional right to **free speech**. In a 7–2 decision, the Court ruled in favor of the students, stating that neither students nor teachers lose their right of expression

58

within the context of a school. Furthermore, the Court argued that the armbands were symbolic in nature and did not pose a disruption to the daily operations of the school. Ultimately, the case established an important precedent for the rights of students and their ability to express themselves in a school setting.

NEW YORK TIMES CO V UNITED STATES

New York Times Co v United States (1971) was an important Supreme Court case that became widely known as the "Pentagon Papers Case." The case reinforced the **freedom of the press** and promoted governmental transparency. The case came about when *The Washington Post* and *The New York Times* attempted to publish the Pentagon Papers, a report by the Defense Department that detailed American involvement in Vietnam and the consequences of continued involvement. When the newspapers in question began to publish the leaked reports, President Richard Nixon (1913–1944) sought a court injunction to suppress their printing. Nixon argued that such an action would compromise national security and that **prior restraint**, or the suppression by the courts of information that may be harmful, was necessary. In a 6–3 decision, the Court ruled against Nixon, stating that prior restraint was unconstitutional unless the government could prove that the material in question would lead to immediate and direct harm to national security. This case ultimately limited government censorship and ensured the protection of the First Amendment.

WISCONSIN V YODER

Wisconsin v Yoder (1972) was a landmark Supreme Court case that upheld the **First Amendment's** protection of religion. The case developed when the State of Wisconsin fined a group of Amish families for failing to enroll their children in high school. The parents argued that the fine, and compulsory education laws in general that required children to attend school beyond eighth grade, violated their religious beliefs. In a unanimous decision, the Supreme Court ruled in favor of the families, stating that Wisconsin's **compulsory education law** violated the **Free Exercise Clause** of the First Amendment, as forcing Amish children to attend high school conflicted with their religious views and way of life. Furthermore, the Court argued that the benefits of additional schooling cited by Wisconsin did not outweigh religious freedom. Ultimately, the ruling reinforced religious protections and also set a precedent for acquiring exemptions for state and federal laws based on religion.

ROE V WADE

Roe v Wade was a controversial 1973 US Supreme Court case. The case originated in 1970 in Texas, which had an **anti-abortion law**. The plaintiff was an unmarried pregnant woman who was assigned the name "Jane Roe" to protect her identity. Texas anti-abortion law characterized the acts of having or attempting to perform an abortion as crimes, with the exception of cases in which an abortion could save the life of a mother. The lawsuit argued that the Texas law was unconstitutionally vague and was not consistent with the rights guaranteed by the First, Fourth, Fifth, Ninth, and Fourteenth Amendments. While the Texas court ruled in favor of Roe, it did not rule that Texas had to discontinue the enforcement of its anti-abortion law. Roe appealed to the Supreme Court in 1971, and the Court's decision in 1973 struck down Texas's abortion laws. The case overturned most state laws prohibiting abortion. In 2022, the Supreme Court reversed its decision in *Roe v Wade*, finding no constitutional basis for requiring states to permit abortion, effectively returning the authority to the states to decide.

UNITED STATES V NIXON

United States v Nixon was a landmark 1974 US Supreme Court case. During the events of the Watergate affair, in which it was revealed that President Nixon's administration was attempting to spy on political opponents, a special prosecutor sought to subpoena audio tapes that contained recordings of Nixon and his administration in the White House. Nixon argued that he could ignore the subpoena, as he had executive privilege as the current president of the United States. Under this executive privilege, he asserted that he had the right to withhold information to protect any confidential information. However, in a unanimous 8–0 decision, the Supreme Court ruled in favor of the special prosecutor, stating that President Nixon must obey the subpoena and release the audio tapes. The Supreme Court stated that presidential privileges are not absolute and cannot be used for generalized confidentiality needs without sufficient cause. This case ultimately led to the resignation of President Nixon and reinforced the principle that a president must be held accountable in the same way as every other US citizen. It set an important precedent limiting the powers of a US president to claim executive privilege, ensuring that future presidents can be held accountable for their actions.

REGENTS OF THE UNIVERSITY OF CALIFORNIA V BAKKE

Regents of the University of California v Bakke was a 1978 Supreme Court case that banned **quota systems** in the college admissions process but ruled that programs providing **advantages to minorities** are constitutionally sound. The case originated when Allan Bakke, a white male who was a strong student, applied to the University of California at Davis Medical School and was rejected. The school had a program that reserved admissions spots for minority applicants; the program had grown along with the overall size of the school since its opening in 1968. Bakke complained to the school but was still not admitted, and he finally brought his case before the Superior Court of California. The California court ruled in favor of Bakke, who claimed that he had been discriminated against because of his race, and the school appealed to the US Supreme Court. The Supreme Court ruled that race could be used as one factor by discriminatory boards such as college admissions boards; however, quotas were ruled to be **discriminatory**.

HAZELWOOD V KUHLMEIER

Hazelwood v Kuhlmeier (1988) was an important case heard by the Supreme Court of the United States pertaining to the **First Amendment** speech rights of students enrolled in public schools. In 1983, a group of students enrolled in Hazelwood School District submitted their student newspaper for approval by the building principal. The principal found two of the articles to be inappropriate and refused to allow them to be printed. Three of the students involved, led by Cathy Kuhlmeier, sued the school district, claiming that their First Amendment rights had been violated. In a 5–3 decision, the Court ruled in favor of the school district, arguing that a school has the right to censor student speech that does not align with its educational mission. As the paper in question was sponsored by the school, it had the authority to limit or edit the material within as long as the actions were guided by valid educational concerns. Ultimately, the case limited the First Amendment rights of students through its differentiation of personal versus school-sponsored expression. Since its inception, this ruling has been used in a variety of ways, ranging from the censoring or limitation of certain types of speech in schools to combating bullying and acts of discrimination within an academic setting.

TEXAS V JOHNSON

Texas v Johnson (1989) was an important Supreme Court case that ruled the burning of the American flag to be a form or expression protected by the First Amendment of the US Constitution (1787). Gregory Lee Johnson burned an American flag outside of the Republican National Convention in Dallas, Texas in 1984. Johnson carried out the act in protest of the polices of President Ronald Reagan and his administration. During that time, Texas and many other states in the union had laws in place that criminalized the desecration of the American flag. Consequently, Johnson was convicted and sentenced to a year in jail and a $2,000 fine. Johnson appealed his conviction to both the Texas Court of Criminal Appeals and the Supreme Court of the United States.

In a 5–4 decision, the Supreme Court ruled in favor of Johnson, arguing that burning a flag is a form of **symbolic speech** that is protected by the First Amendment. Furthermore, the Court stated that the government cannot ban an expression for the sole purpose that others find the act to be offensive. The ruling led to similar laws throughout the United States being overturned, as well as to an unsuccessful attempt to add an amendment banning flag desecration to the US Constitution.

SHAW V RENO

Shaw v Reno (1993) was an important Supreme Court case that outlined the unconstitutionality of racial **gerrymandering**, a process by which the boundaries of electoral districts are drawn to concentrate or dilute voters of a particular race. The process is typically carried out to minimize or maximize voters' influence on elections. Following the 1990 US Census, the State of North Carolina submitted a plan to redistrict its congressional districts based on population shifts. The US Attorney General rejected the plan, as it allowed for only one district in which African Americans constituted the majority. The state revised the plan and resubmitted with the inclusion of one additional African American majority district. The district in question was an irregular shape and did not align with the shape or orientation of other districts. A group of white voters, led by Ruth Shaw, challenged the district, arguing that it was drawn with the sole purpose of incorporating an African American majority and violated the **Equal Protection Clause** of the **Fourteenth Amendment**. When a lower district court ruled that Shaw failed to demonstrate a constitutional violation, the Supreme Court agreed to hear the case. In a 5–4 decision, the Supreme Court ruled in favor of Shaw, arguing that gerrymandering could prove to be unconstitutional if race was the primary factor in drawing the lines and that compelling governmental interest was absent. Furthermore, the Court found that the district in question was drawn in a way that was beyond what should be necessary to combat racial imbalance in the congressional districts. Ultimately, the Court acknowledged that although it may at times be necessary to draw district lines in a way that would combat racial discrepancies, this cannot serve as the sole reason for drawing such lines; any such decisions must be scrutinized to ensure a legitimate purpose.

UNITED STATES V LOPEZ

United States v Lopez (1995) was a landmark Supreme Court case that limited the power of Congress under the **Commerce Clause** of the US Constitution (1787). In 1992, a student named Alfonso Lopez Jr. brought a firearm onto school premises. As a result, he was charged and convicted under the **Gun-Free School Zones Act of 1990**, a piece of federal legislation passed by Congress under the Commerce Clause which prohibited the carrying of firearms on school property. Lopez appealed his conviction, arguing that Congress had overstepped its Constitutional authority in passing the legislation. In a 5–4 decision, the Court ruled in favor of Lopez, stating that Congress had operated outside of its constitutional powers in passing the legislation. Congress had passed the legislation under the Commerce Clause, a section of the Constitution that allows the Legislative Branch the ability to regulate **interstate commerce**. The Court argued that possessing a gun on school property does not constitute an economic activity that may impact interstate commerce. Consequently, the ability of Congress to legislate under the Commerce Clause was limited, and the Gun-Free School Zones Act was deemed unconstitutional.

BUSH V GORE

Bush v Gore (2000) was an important Supreme Court case that ultimately determined the outcome of the 2000 presidential election between George W Bush and Al Gore. The results of the presidential election across the United States were very close, with the victor resting on the outcome in the state of Florida. Florida State law required a machine recount given the incredibly narrow margin (less than 0.5 percent) of victory for Bush in the state. Upon completion of the recount, Bush remained in the lead, with a margin of only 327 votes out of the approximately six

61

million cast in the state. The Florida Supreme Court ordered a hand recount across the state of undervotes, or a paper ballot that had not registered as counting for either candidate. The Bush campaigned sued to stop the recount, stating that different counties across Florida used different standards in counting the ballots, violating the **Equal Protection Clause** of the **Fourteenth Amendment**. In a 7–2 decision, the Court ruled in favor of Bush, arguing that the lack of consistency in counting the ballots resulted in a violation of Equal Protection Clause. The Court also ruled in a 5–4 decision that no recount could take place, as such an act could not be completed in time to meet the safe harbor deadline put in place by the federal government, by which all disputes regarding the selection of presidential electors must be settled. The decision resulted in the awarding of the electoral votes from the State of Florida to Bush, as well as his ultimate victory in the 2000 presidential election.

DISTRICT OF COLUMBIA V HELLER

District of Columbia v Heller (2008) was an important Supreme Court case pertaining to the right to own handguns for self-defense. Washington, DC had very strict gun control laws that included a ban on handguns, as well as a rule that all firearms must be kept unloaded or disassembled. Dick Heller, a police officer in the DC area, applied for a handgun license for the purpose of self-defense. As a police officer, Heller already possessed a permit to carry a handgun while on duty, but he wanted the ability to do so while at home as well. When Heller's application was denied, he sued, arguing that his **Second Amendment** right to keep and bear arms had been violated. In a 5–4 decision, the Court ruled that the Second Amendment protects the rights of individuals, not just militias, to own firearms. Consequently, the Court found that that the handgun restrictions instituted in Washington, DC represented a violation of the Second Amendment and that individuals such as Heller had the right to own firearms for their own protection. Although the case did not negate all gun control legislation, it opened the door for further challenges to gun ownership regulations.

McDONALD V CHICAGO

McDonald v Chicago (2010) was a landmark Supreme Court case that dealt with the application of Second Amendment protections at the state level. Otis McDonald and several other residents of Chicago filed petitions against the cities of Chicago and Oak Park, Illinois. The citizens argued that the strict gun control regulations in place, which effectively banned the ownership of handguns, violated their Second Amendment right to bear arms. Furthermore, the group asserted that the Second Amendment applied not only to the federal government—an outcome which was decided by the earlier case ***District of Columbia v Heller*** **(2008)**—but also to state and local governments through the **Due Process Clause** of the **Fourteenth Amendment**. This clause has been interpreted by the Court to extend the protections provided by the Constitution at the federal level to the state level as well. In a 5–4 decision, the Supreme Court ruled in favor of McDonald, stating that the Second Amendment is applicable to both state and local governments through the Due Process Clause of the Fourteenth Amendment. The case ultimately confirmed the right to bear arms as a fundamental right protected at both the federal and state levels.

CITIZENS UNITED V FEC

Citizens United v Federal Election Commission, or *Citizens United v FEC*, (2010) was a landmark Supreme Court case that tackled the issues of the free speech rights of corporations as well as campaign finance laws. A conservative non-profit organization, Citizens United, planned to air a documentary, *Hillary: The Movie*, that it had produced during the 2008 election cycle. The documentary was critical of Hillary Clinton's ability to serve as President of the United States. Despite the desire of Citizens United to air the documentary, the **Bipartisan Campaign Reform Act (BCRA)** prevented unions and corporations from engaging in **electioneering communications**

within 60 days of a general election or 30 days of a primary election. Consequently, the Federal Election Commission found Citizens United's plan to broadcast ads in support of the documentary to be in violation of BCRA and prevented the organization from proceeding with the planned schedule. Citizens United challenged the decision of the FEC in court. In a 5–4 decision, the Supreme Court ruled in favor of Citizens United, stating that labor unions, corporations, and other organizations bear the same rights to freedom of political speech as individuals. Furthermore, the Court asserted that political spending represents a form of **political speech** and that the expenditures of corporations, unions, and other organizations cannot be limited when it comes to **independent expenditures** on political campaigns. The ruling applied only to independent expenditures, or an expenditure that applies to communication directly in support of or against a candidate, that cannot be made in coordination with any particular candidate. Ultimately, the ruling led to the establishment of Super Political Action Committees (PACS), which can raise unlimited money for a campaign, as long as the PAC is not in direct coordination with the candidate it is supporting.

Landmark Legislation

CONFLICTS AND COMPRISES FACED BY AMERICANS IN THE MID TO LATE 19TH CENTURY

Following the American Revolution, the United States faced a number of challenges. Although the United States and its government have ultimately withstood the test of time, there have been periods of conflict and strife, the first of which developed in the context of establishing the US Constitution (1787). The delegates to the Constitutional Convention struggled to appease the different interest groups that had arisen surrounding issues ranging from slavery to representation to the very structure of the government itself. Furthermore, following the establishment of the Constitution as the governing doctrine of the United States—a document which notably failed to provide a conclusive answer to the issue of slavery—the American people grappled with the legality of the practice of slavery in newly acquired territories. Conversely, members of Congress were forced to compromise on legislative policy in ways that resulted in political and social discord and, ultimately, the Civil War. Despite these conflicts, the United States emerged from the Civil War a unified state, albeit one where former slaves could not fully enjoy the rights provided by the Constitution.

GREAT COMPROMISE

The Great Compromise, also known as the **Connecticut Compromise**, was an important agreement reached at the Constitutional Convention in 1787. At the convention, delegates from large and small states were at odds over political representation in the legislature. Two plans were initially presented at the Constitutional Convention: the **Virginia Plan** and the **New Jersey Plan**. The Virginia plan, drafted by James Madison (1751–1836) and supported primarily by the larger states, proposed a **bicameral** (or two-house) legislature, with representation in the legislature based on population size. Conversely, the **New Jersey Plan**, written by William Patterson (1745–1806), was supported by the smaller states, as it provided for a **unicameral** (or one-house) legislature that offered equal representation for all states regardless of size. The Great Compromise was proposed by Oliver Ellsworth (1745–1807) and Roger Sherman (1721–1793) of Connecticut, and it included the recommendation for a bicameral legislature, with representation in the House of Representatives based on population and representation in the Senate characterized by equal representation regardless for all states. The compromise balanced power between large and small states and ensured that neither would gain an unfair advantage in the legislative process.

Compromise of 1850

The Compromise of 1850 was a series of five laws aimed to reduce tension between the northern and southern states over the issue of slavery after the Mexican-American War (1846–1848). Following the war, the United States gained additional territory from Mexico and faced a period of political turmoil regarding the expansion of slavery into the newly acquired land. Tensions rose exponentially in 1849 when California requested to be admitted to the union as a free state. Representatives from states supporting slavery feared that the admission of another free state would shift the balance of free and slave states in the Senate. The compromise was negotiated primarily by Senator Henry Clay (1777–1852) of Kentucky and included the following five provisions:

- California was to be admitted as a free state, ultimately shifting the balance between free and slave states in the legislature.
- The Fugitive Slave Act was strengthened and required federal and state officials to capture and return escaped slaves. Furthermore, penalties were increased for those who aided escaped slaves.
- The issue of slavery was to be decided by popular vote in the Utah and New Mexico, both of which became official US territories.
- The trade of enslaved peoples in Washington DC was banned; however, the practice of slavery itself was to remain legal there.
- A dispute between Texas and the New Mexico territory was resolved, with Texas relinquishing land claims in exchange for $10 million.

Ultimately, the Compromise of 1850 helped to balance the interests of the free and slave states and delayed the onset of the Civil War (1861–1865).

Kansas-Nebraska Act of 1845

Senator Stephen Douglas of Illinois (1813–1861) introduced the **Kansas-Nebraska Act** to organize the western territories comprising present-day Kansas, Montana, Nebraska, and the Dakotas and to allow for western railroad development. Douglas proposed that the railroads take a northern route through Chicago and other areas in which slavery had been banned by the **Missouri Compromise of 1820**, a statute which banned slavery north of the **36°30′ latitude line**. Consequently, other slave-owning senators preferred the railroad take a southern route through places such as Texas. As a result of the discord, Douglas proposed a compromise in which residents of the new territories would vote to determine if slavery should be allowed. Although this represented a middle-ground approach, it was not enough for the southern representatives, on whom Douglas was reliant for the passage of his bill. These powerful southern senators demanded that the line established by the Missouri Compromise be repealed. Consequently, Douglas introduced a new bill that included the following provisions:

- Two new territories were created: the Kansas and Nebraska Territories.
- The Missouri Compromise was repealed, resulting in the removal of the restriction of slavery north of the 36°30′ latitude line.
- Popular sovereignty was introduced in the territories, allowing settlers to vote on the allowance of slavery.

Ultimately, the Kansas-Nebraska Act reopened the issue of slavery in the United States and its territories, escalated tensions, and led to the Civil War (1861–1865).

CHANGES PERTAINING TO TERRITORIAL EXPANSION AND THE STRUCTURE/FUNCTION OF GOVERNMENT

During the **mid to late 19th century**, the United States underwent a number of changes as it expanded its territory and worked to meet the needs of a growing populace. During this era, the government worked to populate newly acquired territories while juggling the debate over slavery in these locations. Relatedly, the government introduced new measures to allow for regulation of transportation not only in these new territories, but throughout the states already incorporated into the union. Furthermore, the government sought to create a bureaucracy that was educated and qualified to ensure overall fairness and effectiveness. These provisions allowed for the governance of a state with vast territories and a diverse population with varying needs.

HOMESTEAD ACT OF 1862

The Homestead Act of 1862 was an essential piece of legislation that led to greater westward expansion for the United States. The act granted eligible participants 160 acres of free land in the western territories so long as the following requirements were met:

- In order to qualify, the settler was required to be 21 years or older and either already a US citizen or intending to become one. Women were also eligible, and following the Civil War (1861–1865), so were former slaves.
- Settlers were required to live on the allotted land for five years, during which time they were expected to build a home and make improvements to and cultivate the land. After the five-year period, the settlers received the deed to the property.
- If after six months the settler elected to purchase the land as opposed to waiting for the entirety of the five-year period, they were able to do so for a cost of $1.25 per acre.

The Homestead Act of 1862 encouraged westward expansion and helped to provide opportunities for both African Americans and immigrants, who often faced limited opportunities for land ownership on the East Coast.

PENDLETON ACT OF 1883

The Pendleton Act of 1883 was a piece of legislation that established a system that requires employment in the federal civil service to be based on merit. Prior to the passage of the act, civil servants were selected for governmental positions based upon a **spoils system**, in which elected officials appointed their supporters without consideration of their qualifications for the position. The system led to corruption and overall inefficiency across the civil service. The Pendleton Act worked against these issues to develop a hiring and promotion system based on merit for non-elected governmental officials. The primary characteristics of the Pendleton Act include:

- The act requires that governmental positions be filled based on merit and not political affiliation or connections.
- The act introduced protection for federal employees from politically based firings.
- The act created the Civil Service Commission to oversee the merit-based hiring and promotional system.

Although the act initially covered only a small percentage of federal jobs (approximately 10 percent), its scope has ultimately increased, leading to a professional and qualified civil service sector. Despite being amended multiple times since 1883, the Pendleton Act remains in effect and applies to the vast majority of civil service positions within the federal government.

65

INTERSTATE COMMERCE ACT OF 1887

The Interstate Commerce Act of 1887 served as an important piece of legislation aimed at regulating the railroad industry and preventing problematic practices such as monopolies and rate discrimination. In the period following the Civil War (1861–1865), private entities owned railroads, which were largely unregulated. Furthermore, many owners monopolized the area they serviced, and reduced competition allowed them to charge varying fees based on the customer and distance served. The Interstate Commerce Act aimed to rectify these issues and ultimately represented the first governmental attempt to regulate industry in the United States. The act attempted to reduce monopolies, which had become rampant in the railroad industry, by promoting regulation and competition through the enactment of the following provisions:

- The regulation of railroad rates required fair and reasonable pricing so that owners were unable to charge different rates to different customers.
- Railroad owners were required to publicize their rates to ensure fairness and allow for oversight and transparency.
- The creation of the Interstate Commerce Commission (ICC), the first regulatory agency in the United States, which aimed to both oversee and regulate the railroad industry. Railroads were mandated to submit annual reports to the ICC that provided an overview of their operations and finances.

Although limitations existed when it came to the execution of the Interstate Commerce Act, it laid the groundwork for future regulatory agencies and overall intrusion of the government into private industry when required to meet the needs of the American people.

GROWTH AND RESTRICTION OF CIVIL RIGHTS IN THE US IN THE 19TH–21ST CENTURIES

Between the 19th and 21st centuries, US Congress introduced and passed a great deal of legislation, and the Supreme Court ruled on a variety of cases that both expanded and restricted the civil liberties of the American people. Ultimately, these laws and rulings have focused on the changing social, political, and economic needs of the country while balancing both individual and societal needs. Legislation in the 19th century focused on the expansion of civil liberties to marginalized groups and revolved around issues such as slavery, citizenship, and voting rights, while that of the 20th century promoted equity and fairness for groups such as African Americans and women who faced discriminatory practices. The 21st century has brought about new issues for both the Judicial and Legislative Branches to deal with, including debates of over privacy and national security, as well as the balance of power between the personal freedoms of the individual versus the state. In all, each piece of legislation and court ruling highlights the way in which our government and its decisions are ultimately shaped by the political climate of the time.

ALIEN AND SEDITION ACTS OF 1798

When **John Adams** became President, a war was raging between Britain and France. While Adams and the **Federalists** backed the British, Thomas Jefferson and the Republican Party supported the French. The United States nearly went to war with France during this time period, while France worked to spread its international standing and influence under the leadership of **Napoleon Bonaparte**. The **Alien and Sedition Acts** grew out of this conflict and made it illegal to speak in a hostile fashion against the existing government. They also allowed the President to deport anyone in the US who was not a citizen and who was suspected of treason or treasonous activity. When Jefferson became the third President in 1800, he repealed these four laws and pardoned anyone who had been convicted under them.

CIVIL RIGHTS ACT OF 1871

The Civil Rights Act of 1871 was a statute passed following the Civil War. It comprised the **1870 Force Act** and the **1871 Ku Klux Klan Act** and was passed primarily with the intention of protecting Southern black people from the Ku Klux Klan. Since it was passed in 1871, the statute has only undergone small changes. It has, however, been interpreted widely by the courts. In 1882, some parts of the Civil Rights Act of 1871 were found unconstitutional, but the Force Act and the Klan Act continued to be applied in civil rights cases in subsequent years.

FAIR EMPLOYMENT ACT

The Fair Employment Act was signed by President Franklin Roosevelt in 1941. The purpose of this act was to **ban racial discrimination** in industries related to **national defense**, and it represented the very first federal law to ban discrimination in employment. The **Fair Employment Act** mandated that all federal government agencies and departments concerned with national defense, as well as private defense contractors, guaranteed that professional training would be conducted without discrimination based on race, creed, color, or national origin. The Fair Employment Act was followed by **Title VII** of the **1964 Civil Rights Act**, which banned discrimination by private employers, and by **Executive Order 11246** in 1965, which concerned federal contractors and subcontractors.

BOLLING V SHARPE

Bolling v Sharpe was a 1954 Supreme Court case. Like *Brown v Board of Education*, this case addressed issues concerning **segregation in public schools**. The case originated in 1949, when parents from Anacostia, an area in Washington, DC, petitioned the Board of Education of the District of Columbia to allow all races to attend a new school. The request was denied. A lawsuit was brought before the District Court for the District of Columbia on behalf of a student named Bolling and other students to admit them to the all-white school. The case was dismissed by the district court and taken to the Supreme Court. The Supreme Court ruled that the school had to be desegregated based on the Fifth Amendment.

CIVIL RIGHTS ACT OF 1964

The Civil Rights Act of 1964 was passed to protect the rights of both **black men and women**. It served as part of the foundation for the women's rights movement. The act was a catalyst for change in the United States, as it made it illegal to engage in acts of **discrimination** in public facilities, in government, and in employment. The Civil Rights Act of 1964 prohibited unequal voter registration, prohibited discrimination in all public facilities involved in interstate commerce, supported desegregating public schools, ensured equal protection for black people in federally funded programs, and banned employment discrimination.

LOVING V VIRGINIA

Loving v Virginia was a 1967 Supreme Court case that ruled that a particular law in Virginia known as the **Racial Integrity Act of 1924** was unconstitutional, as the law had prohibited interracial marriage. The Supreme Court ruling would put an end to **race-based restrictions on marriage**. The case originated when Mildred Jeter and Richard Loving, an interracial Virginia couple who were married in Washington, DC due to the Virginia state law prohibiting interracial marriage, returned to Virginia and received charges of violating the interracial marriage ban. After pleading guilty, the couple was forced to move to DC to avoid a jail sentence. They brought their case to the Supreme Court on the premise that their Fourteenth Amendment rights had been violated. The Supreme Court found that the Virginia law was unconstitutional and overturned the couple's conviction.

Landmark Supreme Court Cases, Legislation, and Executive Actions

AGE DISCRIMINATION IN EMPLOYMENT ACT (ADEA) OF 1967

The Age Discrimination in Employment Act (ADEA) of 1967 made it illegal for employers to discriminate against people who are **forty years old** or greater in age. The act establishes standards for employer-provided pensions and benefits, and it mandates that information regarding the needs of older workers be made publicly available. In addition to generally banning age discrimination, the **ADEA** specifies particular actions that are illegal. Employers may not specify that individuals of a certain age are preferred or are conversely restricted from applying to job ads. Age limits are only permitted to be mentioned in job ads if age has been shown to be a bona fide occupational qualification. The act stipulates that it is illegal to discriminate based on age through apprenticeship programs and that it is illegal to restrict benefits to older employees. However, employers are permitted to lower the benefits provided to older employees based on age if the expense of providing fewer or lesser benefits is equivalent to the expense of providing benefits to younger employees.

CIVIL RIGHTS ACT OF 1968

The Civil Rights Act of 1968 was passed following the passing of the Civil Rights Act of 1964. This act made it illegal to **discriminate** against individuals during the sale, rental, or financing of **housing**. Therefore, the act is also referred to as the **Fair Housing Act of 1968**. The act made it illegal to refuse to sell or rent housing based on race, color, religion, or national origin. It also made it illegal for anyone advertising housing for sale or rent to specify a preference to rent or sell the property to an individual of a particular race, color, religion, or national origin. In addition, the act ensured protection for civil rights workers.

JONES V MAYER

Jones v Mayer was a 1968 Supreme Court case that ruled that Congress has the authority to **regulate the sale of private property** for the purpose of preventing racial discrimination. This United States Supreme Court ruling was based on a legal statute that stipulates that it is illegal in the United States to commit acts of racial discrimination, both privately and publicly, when selling or renting property. The United States Supreme Court ruled that the congressional power to uphold the statute extends from the power of Congress to uphold the Thirteenth Amendment.

PREGNANCY DISCRIMINATION ACT OF 1978

The Pregnancy Discrimination Act was passed in 1978 as an amendment to the sex discrimination clause of the Civil Rights Act of 1964. The **Pregnancy Discrimination Act** stipulated that people cannot be discriminated against due to pregnancy, childbirth, or medical issues related to pregnancy or childbirth. If a person becomes pregnant, gives birth, or has related medical conditions, that person must receive treatment that is equivalent to that received by other employees, as well as receiving equal benefits as other employees. The **Family and Medical Leave Act** was passed in 1993 to advance protections under the Pregnancy Discrimination Act.

AMERICANS WITH DISABILITIES ACT OF 1990

The Americans with Disabilities Act (ADA) was passed by Congress in 1990. This act outlines the rights of individuals with disabilities in society in all ways besides education. It states that individuals with disabilities should receive **nondiscriminatory treatment** in jobs, **access** to businesses and other stores, and other services. Due to this law, all businesses must be wheelchair accessible, having a ramp that fits the standards of the law, and all doors and bathrooms within those businesses must be able to be used and maneuvered through by someone in a wheelchair. If these rules are not followed, businesses can be subject to large fines until they comply with these

modifications. The ADA also ensures fair treatment when applying for jobs to make sure that there is no unfair discrimination for any person with a disability who is applying for a job.

CIVIL RIGHTS ACT OF 1991

The Civil Rights Act of 1991 is a statute that was passed as a result of a number of Supreme Court decisions that restricted the rights of individuals who had sued their employers on the basis of discrimination. The passing of the **Civil Rights Act of 1991** was the first time since the Civil Rights Act of 1964 was passed that modifications were made to the rights granted under federal laws to individuals in cases involving **employment discrimination**. Specifically, the Civil Rights Act of 1991 granted the right to a trial by jury to individuals involved in cases of employment discrimination, and it also addressed for the first time the potential for emotional distress damages and limited the amount awarded by a jury in such cases.

PLANNED PARENTHOOD V CASEY

Planned Parenthood of Southeastern Pennsylvania v Casey was a 1992 Supreme Court case that challenged the constitutionality of Pennsylvania's abortion laws. The case was brought before the US District Court for the Eastern District of Pennsylvania by abortion clinics and physicians to challenge four clauses of the **Pennsylvania Abortion Control Act of 1982** as unconstitutional under *Roe v Wade*. The district court ruled that all of the clauses of the Pennsylvania act were unconstitutional. The case was then appealed to the Third Circuit Court of Appeals, which ruled to uphold all of the clauses except for one requiring notification of a husband prior to abortion. The case was then appealed to the Supreme Court, which ruled to uphold the constitutional right to have an abortion, thereby upholding *Roe v Wade*.

ADARAND CONSTRUCTORS, INC V PEÑA

Adarand Constructors, Inc v Peña was a 1995 United States Supreme Court case in which the court ruled that any **racial classifications** that are instituted by representatives of federal, state, or local governments must be reviewed and analyzed by a court. The court that reviews such racial classifications must abide by a policy of **strict scrutiny**. Strict scrutiny represents the highest standard of Supreme Court review. Racial classifications are deemed constitutional solely under circumstances in which they are being used as specific measures to advance critical and important governmental interests. The ruling of the Supreme Court in this case, requiring strict scrutiny as a standard of review for racial classifications, overturned the case of *Metro Broadcasting, Inc v FCC*, in which the Supreme Court established a two-level method of reviewing and analyzing racial classifications.

GRUTTER V BOLLINGER

Grutter v Bollinger was a 2003 Supreme Court case that upheld an **affirmative action policy** of the University of Michigan Law School admissions process. The case originated in 1996 when Barbara Grutter, a white in-state resident with a strong academic record, applied to the law school and was denied admission. In 1997, Grutter filed a lawsuit claiming that her rejection was based on racial discrimination and violated her Fourteenth Amendment rights, as well as Title VI of the Civil Rights Act of 1964. The case was heard in 2001 in a US District Court, which ruled that the university's admissions policies were unconstitutional. In 2002, the case was appealed to the Sixth Circuit Court of Appeals, which overturned the lower court's decision. The case was then appealed to the US Supreme Court in 2003, which ruled that the school's affirmative action policy could remain in place, upholding the case of *Regents of the University of California v Bakke* permitting race to be a factor in admissions but banning quotas.

Landmark Supreme Court Cases, Legislation, and Executive Actions

69

NON-DISCRIMINATION ACT (ENDA) AND THE EQUALITY ACT OF 2013

The Employment Non-Discrimination Act was a proposed United States federal law that was introduced various times before Congress but was never passed by both the House and the Senate. The **Employment Non-Discrimination Act** would ban employers from discriminating against their employees based on their **sexual orientation**. A number of states have already passed laws that ban discrimination based on sexual orientation, including California, Connecticut, Hawaii, Maryland, Massachusetts, Minnesota, Nevada, New Hampshire, New Jersey, New Mexico, New York, Rhode Island, Vermont, and Wisconsin. The ENDA has largely been encompassed by a broader resolution known as the Equality Act, which is a bill that would amend the Civil Rights Act of 1964 to further add gender identity and sexual orientation to the list of prohibited categories of discrimination for employment, public accommodations, the jury system, and housing. It has been met with opposition and has not yet been passed by both bodies of Congress.

USA PATRIOT ACT OF 2001

The **USA Patriot Act of 2001** was an important piece of legislation signed into law by George W Bush in response to the terror attacks of September 11, 2001. The act aimed to improve the ability of the US government to both prevent and respond to acts of terrorism through the following provisions:

- It expanded the surveillance abilities of national intelligence and law enforcement agencies by allowing them to wiretap phone calls and electronic communications without requiring a warrant for each form of communication.
- It reduced legal restrictions on property searches through the use of **sneak and peek seizures**, which allowed law enforcement to search a suspect's property without prior notification.
- It provided the government with the ability to violate traditional due process protections through the expedited apprehension and detention of non-US citizens suspected of terrorism, and it expedited their deportation.
- It required financial institutions to provide the government notice of suspicious banking transactions.
- It allowed for easier information-sharing between governmental agencies.

Post 9/11, the Patriot Act was praised for increasing national security and providing the necessary supports to combat future acts of terrorism. At the same time, many critics questioned its infringement on the civil liberties of Americans, especially in the area of due process and privacy rights. While many aspects of the Patriot Act have been allowed to expire, others, such as those pertaining to search warrants, continue to guide law enforcement agencies today.

EXPANSION AND RESTRICTION OF SOCIAL PROGRAMS IN THE US

Social programs—state- and federally funded programs that aim to assist with issues such as healthcare or poverty—in the United States have shifted throughout history, demonstrating periods of both expansion and restriction. Many of these shifts have emerged as a result of political ideology or economic conditions. Typically, social programs aim to meet needs pertaining to poverty, education, unemployment, and healthcare. Although such programs and their growth or restriction can bring about significant impacts on US society, their scope historically depends on the political party and agenda of those in the majority party of the Executive and Legislative Branches of the US government.

THE GREAT SOCIETY

The Great Society can be best understood as a series of programs put into place by **President Lyndon B Johnson** (1908–1973) that aimed to reduce both poverty and racial issues as well as to promote educational improvement and environmental protection in the United States.

- Johnson declared a war on poverty, promising to reduce the poverty rate in the United States. To reach this goal, together with Congress, Johnson introduced a number of programs including **Medicare/Medicaid (1965)**, the **Food Stamp Act (1964)**, and the **Economic Opportunity Act (1964)**.
- The Great Society focused on educational initiatives to improve performance and access to education. The **Elementary and Secondary Education Act of 1965** provided federal funding to low-income schools, while the **Higher Education Act of 1965** sought to make higher education more attainable through the use of federal aid.
- The Johnson administration facilitated several pieces of legislation intended to combat racial inequity. The **Civil Rights Act of 1964** prohibited discrimination based on race, gender, national origin, or religion and banned the practice of segregation in public locations. Furthermore, the **Voting Rights Act of 1965** banned practices that discouraged African Americans from voting, including literacy tests and poll taxes.
- In urban areas, Johnson sought to improve living conditions and promote development. For example, the **Housing and Urban Development Act of 1965** worked to accomplish these goals through revitalization efforts as well as federally funded construction of affordable housing.
- Environmental concerns represented an additional issue on Johnson's agenda. Under Johnson's direction, The **Water Quality Act of 1965** and the **Air Quality Act of 1967** aimed to reduce pollution and ensure the establishment of water quality standards.

The Great Society represents one of the largest attempts in American history to increase social programs and address inequality and resulting socioeconomic issues.

THE NEW DEAL

Franklin Delano Roosevelt (FDR) was elected President in the election of 1932. He was determined to preserve the US government and tried to calm the general public with his folksy "**Fireside Chats**." As the governor of New York, Roosevelt was able to experiment with social welfare programs. He was a pragmatist and a follower of the **Keynesian school of economics**, which insisted that the government had to spend money in order to get out of the Depression. Unlike Hoover, then, Roosevelt supported massive government spending and little volunteerism; he wanted the government to regulate agriculture and industry and for it to take an interest in the daily economic decisions of the people.

In the early days of his term, FDR promoted the **Three Rs**: relief, recovery, and reform. He announced a bank holiday for five days to stop the drain on the cash flow. The **Emergency Banking Act** authorized the **Reconstruction Finance Group** to buy bank stocks in order to finance repair. The **Glass-Steagall Act** made it illegal for banks to loan money to people for the purpose of playing the market and established the **Federal Deposit Insurance Corporation** to protect banks. The **Economy Act** cut $400 million from veterans' payments and $100 million from government salaries. Roosevelt had the gold standard and prohibition repealed. The **Federal Emergency Relief Administration** was established to provide $3 billion in direct relief to people.

The **Civil Works Administration**, headed by Harry Hopkins, was established to create jobs. The **Civilian Conservation Corps** was a civilian army that built infrastructure, such as the Blue Ridge

Landmark Supreme Court Cases, Legislation, and Executive Actions

Parkway. Other organizations created to **employ** people were the Public Works Administration, the Works Progress Administration, the Tennessee Valley Authority (responsible for the construction of 21 dams), the National Youth Administration (which gave work to high school students), and the Rural Electrification Administration. The **National Industrial Recovery Act (NIRA)** was an attempt to encourage fair competition and create scarcity to drive prices up. It established a minimum wage, a maximum number of weekly hours, and the right of labor to organize. In *Schechter Poultry v US* (1935), the Supreme Court would rule that the NIRA should have been made up of laws instead of codes, because there were too many loopholes.

As part of his **New Deal program** to help the US recover from the Great Depression, FDR established the **First Agricultural Adjustment Administration (AAA)**. This agency provided farmers with loans to help them with mortgage payments and paid them to not plant or sell agricultural products. The formation of the **AAA** was economically successful but was one of the least popular measures in the New Deal; it would later be declared unconstitutional in *Butler v US* (1936). The **Federal Securities Act** stated that the securities dealers must disclose the prices of stocks and bonds. The **Wagner Act of 1935** made it illegal for employers to have blacklists of unionized workers. The **Federal Housing Administration** was established to provide lower interest rates for people willing to repair or purchase a house. The **US Housing Authority** was created to loan money to state and local governments for the construction of low-cost housing.

PATIENT PROTECTION AND AFFORDABLE CARE ACT OF 2010

The **Patient Protection and Affordable Care Act of 2010**, known more commonly as the Affordable Care Act, was signed into law by **President Barack Obama** on March 23, 2010, and represented the largest change to the healthcare system in the United States since the inception of Medicaid and Medicare in 1965. The act aimed to increase the affordability of health insurance, reduce the number of uninsured Americans, and improve the healthcare industry as a whole. The Affordable Care Act included several key provisions used to guide the healthcare industry:

- It required all Americans to have healthcare. This policy, known as an **individual mandate**, forces uninsured Americans to pay an additional tax to the government.
- It established a state-based health insurance marketplace in which individuals have the ability to shop for coverage options.
- It expanded Medicaid so that more low-income adults were covered. This requirement was ultimately ruled to be at the discretion of each individual state.
- It forced employers with 50 or more employees to provide health insurance to their workforce.
- It banned healthcare providers from discriminating against individuals with pre-existing conditions.
- It mandated the coverage of preventative screenings such as vaccines or cancer screens.
- It allowed young adults to remain on the health insurance of their parents until the age of 26.

The Affordable Care Act greatly reduced the number of uninsured Americans and greatly altered the healthcare industry in the United States.

LEGISLATION PERTAINING TO ENVIRONMENTAL PROTECTION

Several pieces of legislation pertaining to environmental protection have shaped US governmental policy in areas such as combatting pollutants, managing natural resources, and protecting the environment overall.

- **The National Environmental Policy Act (1969)** represents the first significant environmental law in the United States. The act requires that all federal agencies consider the environmental implication of large-scale projects like the construction of highways. It requires that Environmental Impact Statements are prepared to detail any potential environmental implications.
- **The Clean Air Act of 1970** represents an essential piece of environmental legislation that sought to reduce pollution and improve air quality. The act authorized the Environmental Protection Agency (EPA) to establish air quality standards across the United States to limit harmful pollutants and reduce emissions from both industrial sources and vehicles. Furthermore, the Clean Air Act required states to develop plans to meet the new standards.
- **The Clean Water Act of 1972** focuses on the control of pollutants in the nation's waters. The act established quality standards for surface waters and focused on the prevention of industrial discharge of pollutants, as well as runoff from land used for agriculture. Additionally, the act assists wastewater treatment plants with the disposal of hazardous materials.

Ultimately, the administration of these pieces of legislation is overseen by the EPA, which focuses on the implementation of environmental policies throughout the United States.

HOW PRESIDENTIAL POWER HAS INCREASED SINCE THE DRAFTING OF THE US CONSTITUTION

As the United States government has evolved since the ratification of the US Constitution in 1788, the power of the Executive Branch has increased significantly. Although the Constitution details specific executive powers, interpretation of such powers has changed, leading to a more powerful Executive Branch. This has proven especially true during times of war or other crises. Several examples exist that demonstrate the expansion of executive power in periods of conflict.

- **Korean War (1950–1953)**: In the lead-up to the Korean War, Americans were terrified of the spread of communism, and the US government sought to limit its spread through a policy of containment. The Korean War represented the first true test of such a policy. President Harry S Truman elected to send troops to Korea to protect South Koreans from aggression by a communist-led North Korean state. Truman carried out this goal without an explicit declaration of war from Congress, instead claiming that his ability to do so was outlined in his constitutional powers as commander-in-chief of the armed forces as part of the larger goal of containing the spread of communism. Furthermore, Truman claimed that American involvement was part of an act led by the United Nations (UN) and supported by UN resolution. Ultimately, this decision expanded the scope of executive power, with many questioning the constitutionality of Truman's actions.

Landmark Supreme Court Cases, Legislation, and Executive Actions

Copyright © Mometrix Media. You have been licensed one copy of this document for personal use only. Any other reproduction or redistribution is strictly prohibited. All rights reserved. This content is provided for test preparation purposes only and does not imply an endorsement by Mometrix of any particular political, scientific, or religious point of view.

- **Tonkin Gulf Resolution:** In 1964, during the Vietnam War, Congress passed the Tonkin Gulf Resolution to provide President Lyndon B Johnson the power to utilize expanded military forces in Vietnam without a formal congressional declaration of war. Several purported acts of aggression occurred in Vietnam in the days leading up to the passage of the resolution, leading to Congress authorizing expanded military presence in Vietnam as well as an ultimate increase in presidential power. Although these acts of aggression were ultimately found to be exaggerated, they assisted in the establishment of a precedent in which the scope of the Executive Branch's power was increased in the areas of military and foreign policy.
- **Authorization for Use of Military Force (2001):** The events of September 11, 2001, led to further expansion of executive power. On September 18, 2001, the Authorization for Use of Military Force (AUMF) was passed in joint resolution by Congress. The resolution allowed President George W Bush to use broad military power against those responsible for the events of 9/11. The resolution served as the legal backing for many counterterror operations in the years that followed. Although initially intended to be used against the perpetrators of the terror attacks of 9/11, the resolution has been used to justify military operations in over 20 countries around the world.

These pieces of legislation demonstrate how executive military power is often greatly expanded in times of strife, ultimately superseding the checks and balances established in the Constitution.

Landmark Executive Actions

HISTORY OF US FOREIGN POLICY

Upon the establishment of the United States as a sovereign, independent state, governmental officials quickly learned the importance of navigating the world stage, developing a system of **foreign policy** that continues to evolve today. Early foreign policy established the United States as a primary source of influence within the Western Hemisphere and dictated the terms of engagement with the European powers. As time progressed, the United States sought to expand its territory, both throughout the United States and beyond, through a series of treaties and purchases. US foreign policy has also focused on diplomacy; the US has brokered and been a part of treaties aimed to end military conflict on a global and regional basis.

MONROE DOCTRINE

The **Monroe Doctrine**, established by President James Monroe in 1823, highlighted an early American foreign policy goal to limit European involvement in the Western Hemisphere. Monroe theorized that Europe and the United States should have separate spheres of influence, and he declared that any attempt by European nations to colonize or interfere in general in the Americas would be viewed by the United States as an act of aggression. Furthermore, Monroe stated that the United States would not interfere in the operations of Europe. Although the initial purpose of the Monroe Doctrine was to prevent European involvement in areas geographically near the United States, it ultimately laid the groundwork for US intervention in Latin America throughout the 19th and 20th centuries and remains a key element of US foreign policy in the Western Hemisphere. Ultimately, the United States continues to serve as a primary power in the Western Hemisphere, a position stemming from the introduction of the Monroe Doctrine.

TREATIES/AGREEMENTS THAT THE US HAS DEVELOPED OR PARTICIPATED IN DEVELOPING

The United States has a rich history of engaging in treaties and other agreements to end armed conflict both domestically and abroad. These treaties have included some that have resulted in the end of global conflicts, while others have addressed conflicts impacting the United States domestically or on a regional basis.

- **Treaty of Paris (1783)** was an important treaty signed by Great Britain and the United States that ended the American Revolutionary War (1775–1783) and was based on a preliminary treaty signed in 1782. The Treaty of Paris formally established the United States as a sovereign state, free from British rule, and it laid the boundaries between the United States and the British colonial state in the north (present-day Canada).
- **Treaty of Guadalupe Hidalgo (1848)** served as an important treaty between the United States and Mexico that officially ended the Mexican-American War (1846–1848). The treaty resulted in Mexico relinquishing approximately 55 percent of its territory, including that of present-day California, Utah, New Mexico, Nevada, and portions of Kansas, Wyoming, and Oklahoma. In turn, the United States paid Mexico a sum of $15 million. The treaty greatly expanded US territory and helped shape the borders of the modern-day United States of America.
- **Treaty of Versailles (1919)** was an essential treaty that ended World War II (1914–1918) and required Germany to face territorial losses and pay heavy reparations for its involvement in the conflict. Although the United States helped shape the peace terms of the treaty, the US Senate refused to ratify it. Many Americans were fearful that by ratifying the treaty, and ultimately joining the League of Nations, the US would be dragged into European armed conflicts in the future.
- **Korean Armistice Agreement (1953)** was not representative of a true treaty ratified by Congress, but it ended fighting on the Korean Peninsula, effectively ending the Korean War (1950–1953). The agreement was signed by the United Nations Command (led by the United States), North Korea, and China and established a ceasefire between forces representing North and South Korea. The agreement created a **demilitarized zone (DMZ)** on the **38th parallel** between North and South Korea. Although fighting ended as a result of the agreement, the two states still technically remain at war, as no official treaty was ever signed.

These treaties and agreements have resolved conflict, promoted peace, and helped to shape US foreign policy both at home and abroad.

TERRITORIAL EXPANSION IN THE US AND ITS PRIMARY JUSTIFICATION

Territorial expansion can be best understood as a period in US history in which the nation's borders expanded significantly. In general, military conflicts, treaties, and large-scale land purchases contributed to territorial expansion, but this growth was ultimately facilitated by belief in the principal of **Manifest Destiny**. Manifest Destiny was the belief that territorial expansion was destined or ordained by God and that it was the responsibility of the United States of America to spread both democratic and capitalist ideals throughout North America. Ultimately, this principle drove westward expansion during the 19th century and was used to justify the removal of Native Americans from their land. Furthermore, territorial expansion contributed to conflict regarding slavery, as the states were divided over whether to permit slavery in the newly acquired territories.

TERRITORIAL EXPANSION IN THE US

DURING THE EARLY 19TH CENTURY

Territorial expansion in the early 19th century focused on expansion to the southern and western parts of North America.

- **Louisiana Purchase (1803):** The Louisiana Purchase represented a deal in which the United States purchased approximately 827,000 square miles west of the Mississippi River from France for a price of $15 million. The acquisition doubled the size of the United States and laid the groundwork for future expansion.
- **Florida Acquisition (1819):** Also known as the Adams-Onis Treaty, the Florida Acquisition was a treaty between Spain and the United States in which Spain ceded Florida to the US in exchange for the US assuming the repayment of claims made against the Spanish government. Additionally, the treaty determined the boundary between US and Spanish territories in New Spain (modern-day Mexico).

Ultimately, the Louisiana Purchase and Adams-Onis Treaty significantly contribute to the growth of the United States while also reiterating the notion that US foreign policy revolved around expansionist goals.

DURING THE MID-19TH CENTURY

US territorial expansion in the mid-19th century focused primarily on land previously held by Texas, as well as some held by Great Britain, to a lesser degree.

- **Texas Annexation (1845):** The Texas Annexation occurred when Texas, which had secured independence from Spain in 1836, became the 28th US state. Although Texas had originally applied for statehood following their independence, the United States initially declined, fearful of conflict with Spain, who refused to acknowledge Texan independence. Upon official ratification of Texas as a state, increased tensions with Spain emerged, leading to the Mexican-American War in 1846.
- **Oregon Treaty (1846):** The Oregon Treaty was a treaty signed by the United States and Great Britain that resolved a dispute regarding a large territory in the Pacific Northwest claimed by both states. The treaty established the 49th parallel as the official dividing point of the United States and British Canada between the Pacific Ocean and Rocky Mountains, with the United States gaining control of most of the territory in question.
- **Mexican Cession (1848):** The Mexican Cession occurred in the context of the Treaty of Guadalupe Hidalgo in 1848, which formally ended the Mexican-American War. Mexico ceded a great deal of land to the United States in exchange for $15 million.
- **Gadsden Purchase (1853):** The Gadsden purchase was an agreement between the United States and Mexico in which the United States gain approximately 29,000 square miles in present-day New Mexico and Arizona at a cost of $10 million. The acquisition helped to settle a border dispute between Mexico and the United States, and it allowed for greater US expansion.

These territorial expansions greatly increased the scope of US influence and territory in general, while also solving disputes between the US and foreign states.

76

DURING THE LATE 19TH AND EARLY 20TH CENTURIES

Throughout the late 19th and early 20th centuries, the United States continued to expand its territory through a variety of treaties and general purchases from other foreign powers.

- **Alaska Purchase (1867):** The Alaska Purchase was a treaty signed between the United States and Russia in which the US attained Alaska in exchange for a payment of $7.2 million to Russia. Although the treaty was initially ridiculed, the acquisition later proved to be lucrative due to Alaska's wealth of natural resources such as gold and oil deposits.
- **Hawaiian Annexation (1898):** In 1898, the United States annexed Hawaii following the Newland Resolution, which recognized Hawaii as a US territory. The resolution followed the overthrow of the Kingdom of Hawaii in 1893 and the installation of a provisional government supported by the United States. The annexation expanded US presence in the Pacific Ocean and supported the economic interests of the United States.
- **Spanish-American War and Treaty of Paris (1898):** The Treaty of Paris formally ended the Spanish-American War (1898) and allowed for US acquisition of oversees territory including Guam, the Philippines, and Puerto Rico. The treaty also led to Cuban independence from Spain, although the United States maintained influence over the state through the Platt Agreement.
- **The Treaty of the Danish West Indies (1917):** In 1917, the United States acquired the US Virgin Islands from Denmark in exchange for $25 million. The acquisition was motivated by World War I (1914–1918), as the United States hoped to attain an advantage in military defense, for which the Caribbean was seen as an essential.

Ultimately, territorial expansion in the late 19th and early 20th centuries was focused on expanding American territory beyond the borders of the continental United States.

EXPANSION AND RESTRICTION OF CIVIL LIBERTIES THROUGHOUT US HISTORY

Throughout the course of US history, civil liberties have been both expanded and restricted. The government's power to restrict civil rights is typically used in times of crisis, such as wartime, when the government may limit liberties for the purpose of national security. Conversely, the government has also expanded the civil liberties of the American people during periods of societal change through Supreme Court rulings.

- **Suspensions of Habeas Corpus:** Habeas corpus, or the right of individuals to challenge their imprisonment, has been suspended during times of national crisis, ultimately restricting important civil liberties. For example, during the Civil War (1861–1865), Abraham Lincoln (1809–1865) suspended habeas corpus so that individuals suspected of supporting the confederacy could be arrested and detained without access to a speedy trial.
- **Japanese American Internment:** In 1942, following the attack on Pearl Harbor by Japan—an event which brought the United States into World War II (1939–1945)—the US government forced the internment of over 100,000 Japanese Americans through Executive Order 9066. This order required that Japanese Americans be relocated and confined to internment camps, a violation of many important civil liberties including due process, the ability to move freely, and the right to own property.
- **Enforcement of Civil Rights:** Supreme Court decisions have played a significant role in expanding civil rights to all US citizens, especially those from minority groups. For example, *Brown v Board of Education* (1954) banned the practice of segregation in schools, deeming it unconstitutional, and assisted in promoting racial equality across the United States.

Although the US Constitution (1787) and Bill of Rights provide for the protection of many civil liberties, during certain periods of time those rights have been either suspended or expanded in attempts to provide protection to more US citizens.

USE OF EXECUTIVE ORDERS BY PREVIOUS US PRESIDENTS

An executive order represents a directive by the President of the United States that allows for the management of the federal government. Such an order allows the President to carry out the constitutional power to ensure the faithful execution of laws. Executive orders carry the weight of law, but they may be challenged in the judicial system or overturned by future Presidents. Many important executive orders have been carried out throughout US history, with each President typically signing off on a number throughout his term.

- **Desegregation of the military:** Executive orders played an important role in the desegregation of the military. President Harry S Truman issued Executive Order 9981 in 1948, banning the use of racial segregation within units and requiring fair and equal treatment for all military personnel regardless of race. The order also established the President's Committee on Equality on Treatment and Opportunity, which was designed to oversee the implementation of the policy.
- **Affirmative action:** Affirmative action can be best understood as a series of policies that work to prevent discrimination based on race, gender, or other defining characteristics in various sectors such as college admissions or employment. Several Presidents have utilized executive orders to promote affirmative action. For example, President John F Kennedy issued Executive Order 10925 to develop the President's Committee on Equal Employment Opportunity, as well as to require that federal contractors take affirmative action to provide equitable employment opportunities to those from minority groups.

Beyond the scope of desegregation of the military and affirmative action, Presidents have utilized executive orders to address many policy issues without congressional oversight.

USE OF THE PRESIDENTIAL "BULLY PULPIT" IN AMERICAN HISTORY

Coined by President Theodore Roosevelt, the term **"bully pulpit"** can be best understood as the use of presidential power and unique influence to promote an agenda and influence the opinion of the public. Roosevelt used the word "bully" as a means to describe a position of strength or power, and the term did not have the negative connotation that is applied to it in more modern times. Presidents have used the "bully pulpit" to accomplish a variety of goals throughout the 20th and 21st centuries. For example, President Franklin D Roosevelt (1882–1945) utilized his **fireside chats**, informal conversations broadcast on the radio, to speak directly to the people and break down the policies associated with the **New Deal**, simplifying their social and economic outcomes. Additionally, President Barack Obama also called upon the notion of the "bully pulpit" to achieve his agenda. When attempting to garner support for the **Affordable Care Act (2010)**, Obama engaged in a number of town hall speeches, made media appearances, and delivered speeches aimed at directly convincing his constituents that the health care industry required significant changes. Ultimately, the position awarded to the President of the United States allows for an increased ability to advocate for programs or issues of personal importance through direct communication with the populace.

WAR POWERS GRANTED TO THE PRESIDENT OF THE UNITED STATES

The war powers of the President of the United States originate primarily in the United States Constitution (1787). The Constitution provides the President with the power to serve as commander-in-chief of the armed forces, while the United States Congress holds the power to formally declare war. Consequently, it is important to note that although the President has the ability to carry out a variety of tasks, such as the ability to respond to immediate threats, or to direct military forces overall, only Congress may officially approve military engagement. That being said, throughout history Presidents have pushed the boundaries regarding their use of military force, often citing immediate concerns to protect the United States and its people. For example, President Harry S Truman (1884–1972) sent troops to Korea in the Korean War (1950–1953) without an explicit declaration of war from Congress. Truman claimed his ability to do so was outlined in his constitutional powers as commander-in-chief of the armed forces as part of the larger goal of containing the spread of communism. Ultimately, Presidents of the 20th and 21st centuries have expanded the scope of executive war powers setting precedents for future leaders of the Executive Branch.

Landmark Supreme Court Cases, Legislation, and Executive Actions

FCLE Practice Test #1

1. Guaranteed rights enumerated in the Declaration of Independence, possessed by all people, are referred to as:

    a. Universal rights
    b. Unalienable rights
    c. Voting rights
    d. Peoples' rights

2. Who was the main author of the Bill of Rights?

    a. George Washington
    b. John Adams
    c. Thomas Jefferson
    d. James Madison

3. The First Amendment to the Constitution deals mainly with which of the following?

    a. The right of free expression
    b. The right to a speedy and public trial
    c. Protection from cruel and unusual punishment
    d. Freedom from unreasonable search and seizure

4. Under the Articles of Confederation, which of the following was Congress NOT granted the power to do?

    a. Wage war and make treaties
    b. Regulate Indian affairs
    c. Appoint military officers
    d. Levy taxes

5. Historian Richard B. Morris identified seven men among the many identified as Founding Fathers of the United States who were most important in forming our nation. These seven included George Washington, Thomas Jefferson, and Benjamin Franklin. Whom of the following did he not include in the rest of the seven?

    a. Patrick Henry
    b. John Adams
    c. John Jay
    d. James Madison

6. What group petitions the government?

    a. Common Cause
    b. Party leaders
    c. Lobbyists
    d. Party activists

7. One of the earliest political parties in the United States was the Federalist Party. Its decline is best explained by:
  a. A failure to organize state political parties
  b. The enmity of wealthy Americans
  c. Its opposition to the War of 1812
  d. Its advocacy of a strong central government

8. To be President of the United States, one must meet these three requirements:
  a. The President must be college educated, at least 30 years old, and a natural citizen.
  b. The President must be a natural citizen, have lived in the US for 14 years, and have a college education.
  c. The President must be a natural citizen, be at least 35 years old, and have lived in the US for 14 years.
  d. The President must be at least 30 years old, be a natural citizen, and have lived in the US for 14 years.

9. _____ is considered the primary author of the Federalist Papers.
  a. George Clinton
  b. Alexander Hamilton
  c. Robert Yates
  d. John Jay

10. Under the United States Constitution, the power to tax and borrow is:
  a. Implied
  b. Shared
  c. Expressed
  d. Reserved

11. What does nationalism accomplish?
  a. Nationalism legitimizes authority and establishes unity
  b. Nationalism creates chaos
  c. Nationalism causes division
  d. Nationalism causes people to question their leaders

12. To whom was the Declaration of Independence addressed and why?
  a. To the British Parliament because the colonists were opposed to being ruled by a king who had only inherited his throne and only considered the popularly elected Parliament to hold any authority over them
  b. To the King of England because the colonists were upset that Parliament was passing laws for them even though they did not have the right to elect members of Parliament to represent their interests
  c. To the governors of the rebelling colonies so that they would know that they had 30 days to either announce their support of the Revolution or to return to England
  d. To the colonial people as a whole because the Declaration of Independence was intended to outline the wrongs that had been inflicted on them by the British military and inspire them to rise up in protest

13. Which one of these landmark Supreme Court decisions involving the right to an attorney took place sometime after the Cold War?

a. *Gideon v. Wainwright*
b. *Montejo v. Louisiana*
c. *Escobedo v. Illinois*
d. *Miranda v. Arizona*

14. What was the purpose of the Mayflower Compact?

a. To create and enact a series of laws for the Pilgrims.
b. To create a temporary government for the Pilgrims.
c. To memorialize the Pilgrims' promises to raise their children according to their religious ideals.
d. To memorialize the laws under which the Pilgrims had previously been living

15. Which statement best describes how the 1896 US Supreme Court decision in *Plessy v. Ferguson* most influenced US society?

a. It reinforced the rights of individual states.
b. It legalized poll taxes and similar measures.
c. It provided a legal basis for racial segregation.
d. It determined the legality of railway strikes.

16. Which of the following events happened earliest on the eve of the American Revolution?

a. The Declaration of Independence, drafted mainly by Thomas Jefferson, was officially taken up by America's Second Continental Congress.
b. Thomas Paine published his famous pamphlet, *Common Sense*, influencing even more moderate Americans to agree upon independence.
c. The Second Continental Congress issued the "Olive Branch Petition," begging King George III to ask Parliament to make peace with them.
d. King George III of England approved the Prohibitory Act, an official declaration that the colonists were in rebellion and no longer protected.

17. The United States Congress funds Amtrak, a national railroad system. Railroads did not exist when the framers wrote the Constitution. However, this use of funds is legal and is covered in Article 1 of the Constitution as

a. a delegated power.
b. a denied power.
c. an expressed power.
d. an implied power.

18. Which constitutional requirement for passing a bill rarely happens?

a. The leader of the majority party decides when to place the bill on the calendar for consideration before Congress
b. The versions of a bill that pass through both houses of Congress and are signed by the President must have the exact same wording
c. The number and kind of amendments introduced in the House are limited
d. A filibuster needs a supermajority vote to be broken

19. The power of Congress to override a Presidential veto is an example of:

a. Checks and balances
b. Separation of powers
c. Judicial review
d. Advice and consent

20. How many Vice Presidents have succeeded as President?

a. Four
b. Thirteen
c. Nine
d. Five

21. The primary expense for most state and local governments is:

a. Emergency medical services
b. Transportation services
c. Police and fire departments
d. Education

Refer to the following for question 22:

ARTICLE XXVII (Ratified July 1, 1971)

Section 1. The right of citizens of the United States, who are eighteen years of age or older, to vote shall not be denied or abridged by the United States or by any State on account of age.

22. This amendment to the Constitution was ratified in part because of what historic moment?

a. Women gained the right to vote.
b. Suffrage was extended to all African Americans.
c. Young men were being drafted to serve in the Vietnam War.
d. The number of people under 21 years of age increased.

23. The vice president succeeds the president in case of death, illness or impeachment. What is the order of succession for the next three successors, according to the Presidential Succession Act of 1947?

a. President pro tempore of the Senate, secretary of state, and secretary of defense
b. Speaker of the House, president pro tempore of the Senate, and secretary of state
c. President pro tempore of the Senate, Speaker of the House, and secretary of state
d. Secretary of state, secretary of defense, and Speaker of the House

24. The Federal Deposit Insurance Corporation (FDIC) and the Securities and Exchange Commission (SEC) were created during whose presidency?

a. Theodore Roosevelt
b. Woodrow Wilson
c. Franklin Roosevelt
d. Harry Truman

25. Which of the following represents one of the primary arguments presented by the Anti-Federalists in the lead-up to the ratification of the US Constitution?

    a. A strong federal government was needed to address the weaknesses of the Articles of Confederation.

    b. The proposed system of government would prevent commerce from being effectively regulated.

    c. The new Constitution provided too much power to the federal government at the expense of state sovereignty.

    d. A federal system of government would ensure a balance of power between the federal and state governments.

26. Which is NOT a constitutional responsibility of the president of the United States?

    a. Negotiating treaties with Senate approval

    b. Recommending legislation

    c. Choosing chairpersons for standing committees of Congress

    d. Seeking counsel of cabinet secretaries

27. Criminal cases are tried under:

    I. State law
    II. Federal law
    III. Civil court

    a. I and III

    b. II only

    c. I only

    d. I and II

28. What are the official requirements for becoming a senator?

    a. A senator must be at least 35 years old, a US citizen for a minimum of seven years, and a resident of the state he represents.

    b. A senator must be at least 30 years old, a US citizen for a minimum of nine years, and a resident of the state he represents.

    c. A senator must be at least 25 years old, a US citizen for a minimum of nine years, and a resident of the state and district he represents.

    d. A senator must be at least 30 years old, a natural citizen, and a resident of the state he represents.

29. Which of the following is not a result of the Civil Rights Movement's work in the 1950s and 60s?

    a. The government enacted legislation prohibiting racial discrimination in employment.

    b. Disenfranchisement of African Americans was declared illegal.

    c. Court rulings that segregation in schools violated the Constitution led to a near instantaneous desegregation of public educational facilities.

    d. The government enacted legislation prohibiting racial discrimination in the housing market.

30. What does the term "en banc" mean?

    a. A document requesting an appeal

    b. A petition to the Supreme Court

    c. A larger group of judges who review an appellate court's decision

    d. The legal argument of an appellant

31. The Head of State and Chief Executive are two separate offices in which system?
   a. Presidential system
   b. Authoritarian system
   c. Parliamentary system
   d. Representative democracy

32. The Nineteenth Amendment expanded voting rights to which of the following groups?
   a. Non-landowning men
   b. Women
   c. African Americans
   d. Residents of US territories

33. The President has the power to veto legislation. How is this power limited?
   I. Congress can override the veto
   II. The President cannot line veto
   III. The President cannot propose legislation
   a. I and III
   b. II only
   c. I and II
   d. I only

34. Which group(s) of people were originally responsible for selecting the members of the US Senate?
   a. State legislatures
   b. State governors
   c. State electors
   d. State residents, subject to voting eligibility

35. Which of the following was a provision of the Northwest Ordinance of 1787 that influenced the development of the United States as a constitutional republic?
   a. It designated newly admitted states as subordinate to previously admitted states for a period of five years.
   b. It outlined a system of taxation that required the newly acquired territories to support the state.
   c. It developed a process by which territories could achieve statehood and be admitted to the United States.
   d. It established armed forces in the newly acquired territories to control uprisings.

36. The writers of *The Federalist Papers* published under the pen name "Publius." Who were the authors?
   a. James Madison, John Jay, and Alexander Hamilton
   b. George Washington, Thomas Jefferson, and James Madison
   c. Alexander Hamilton, Benjamin Franklin, and Thomas Jefferson
   d. Benjamin Franklin, John Jay, and Thomas Jefferson

37. What are the official requirements for serving in the House of Representatives?

    a. Members of the House must be at least 30 years old, a US citizen for a minimum of nine years, and a resident of the state and district they represent.

    b. Members of the House must be at least 25 years old, a natural citizen, and a resident of the state they represent.

    c. Members of the House must be at least 30 years old, a natural citizen, and a resident of the state and district they represent.

    d. Members of the House must be at least 25 years old, a US citizen for a minimum of seven years, and a resident of the state they represent.

38. What is the power of the President to veto an act of Congress an example of?

    a. Checks and balances
    b. Separation of powers
    c. Judicial review
    d. Advice and consent

39. What are the first ten amendments to the Constitution more commonly known as?

    a. The Civil Rights Act
    b. Common law
    c. The Equal Protection clause
    d. The Bill of Rights

40. Of the following, which person or group was NOT instrumental in advancement of civil rights and desegregation during the 1940s and 1950s?

    a. The President
    b. The Supreme Court
    c. The Congress
    d. The NAACP

41. Enlightenment principles signaled a departure from which of the following types of government rule?

    a. Monarchy
    b. Democracy
    c. Anarchy
    d. Republicanism

42. Virginian _____ advocated a stronger central government and was influential at the Constitutional Convention.

    a. Benjamin Franklin
    b. James Madison
    c. George Mason
    d. Robert Yates

43. Most federal judges have served as local judges, lawyers, and law professors. These are _____ qualifications.

    a. Formal
    b. Required
    c. Informal
    d. Recommended

44. Disagreements between individuals or organizations are tried in:
   a. Civil court
   b. Criminal court
   c. Federal court
   d. State court

45. Which Supreme Court case enforced the civil rights of citizens to not incriminate themselves?
   a. Marbury v. Madison
   b. Miranda v. Arizona
   c. Youngstown Sheet and Tube Company v. Sawyer
   d. United States v. Carolene Products Company

46. How is the jurisdiction of federal courts usually decided?
   a. By the president
   b. By Congress
   c. By the voters
   d. By the Supreme Court

47. How many members of the Electoral College represent Washington, D.C.?
   a. One
   b. Two
   c. Three
   d. Five

48. The United States Constitution was most significantly influenced by which of the following movements?
   a. The Enlightenment
   b. The Industrial Revolution
   c. The Neolithic Revolution
   d. The Renaissance

49. Who did NOT write about the concept of the Social Contract, which was incorporated into the Declaration of Independence?
   a. Thomas Hobbes
   b. John Locke
   c. Jean-Jacques Rousseau
   d. Benjamin Franklin

50. How did the Truman Doctrine shape US foreign policy after World War II?
   a. It influenced President Truman's decision to create commissions on civil rights.
   b. It shaped the US role in rebuilding the economies of postwar Europe.
   c. It led the US government to refrain from interfering with the US economy.
   d. It led to US military involvement in countries such as Korea.

FCLE Practice Test #1

51. The philosophy of the late 17th-18th centuries that influenced the Constitution was from the Age of:

   a. Enlightenment
   b. Empire
   c. Discovery
   d. Industry

52. In 1957, President Dwight Eisenhower sent federal troops to Little Rock, Arkansas. They were to enforce integration at Little Rock Central High School, although the governor of the state had tried to prevent integration. Eisenhower's action is an example that illustrates:

   a. Showing a governor that he had no real power in state government
   b. Trying to keep federal troops out of Vietnam
   c. States' rights being more important than federal law
   d. Upholding federal law if state or local officials will not

53. In 1890, the US government passed the Sherman Antitrust Act. The Act has been most influential in restricting anticompetitive practices by:

   a. Outlawing acts that restrained interstate trade
   b. Its use in dissolving the Standard Oil trust
   c. Outlawing acts that restrained intrastate trade
   d. By its use in dissolving the AT&T monopoly

54. Which of the following is true concerning the formation of new state governments in the United States of America following freedom from British rule?

   a. By the end of 1777, new constitutions had been created for twelve of the American states.
   b. The states of Connecticut and Massachusetts retained their colonial charters, minus the British parts.
   c. The state of Massachusetts required a special convention for its constitution, setting a good example.
   d. The state of Massachusetts did not formally begin to use its new constitution until 1778.

55. What does *due process* mean?

   a. It's important for every citizen to follow the laws of their state and country.
   b. Any accused person may confront the accuser and provide a defense.
   c. Capital punishment is appropriate if a person is convicted of murder.
   d. An accused person is considered guilty until proven to be innocent.

56. In LBJ's Great Society program, which of the following was NOT included?

   a. Medicare
   b. Voting rights
   c. Federal aid to education
   d. Ending the Vietnam War

57. Reference the excerpt below from the Massachusetts Constitution to answer the question that follows.

> All men are born free and equal, and have certain natural, essential, and unalienable rights; among which may be reckoned the right of enjoying and defending their lives and liberties; that of acquiring, possessing, and protecting property; in fine, that of seeking and obtaining their safety and happiness.

Source: General Court of the Commonwealth of Massachusetts

The text included above most likely influenced the framers in their development of which section of the United States Constitution?

a. Article I
b. Article II
c. Article III
d. The Bill of Rights

58. Which statement best describes the significance of the Mayflower Compact on colonial America?

a. It declared that the colonists were independent from King James.
b. It served as a blueprint for the later Bill of Rights.
c. It provided the Pilgrims the first written basis for laws in the New World.
d. It established Puritanism as the official religion for Puritan colonies.

59. The annexation of Texas by the United States in 1845 is best described as of which of the following?

a. An effort to help stem the spread of slavery west of the Mississippi
b. Part of an effort to fulfill Manifest Destiny
c. An expression of principles set forth in the Monroe Doctrine
d. An effort to improve relations between the United States and Mexico

60. What did the landmark Supreme Court case, *Brown v. The Board of Education of Topeka* decide?

a. That school busing was inherently Constitutional.
b. That the doctrine of separate but equal was Unconstitutional.
c. That racially separate educational facilities deprive people of equal protection under the laws.
d. That Plessy v. Ferguson was appropriately decided.

61. Proponents of legislating greater societal income equity support all of the following EXCEPT:

a. Impose a progressive income tax
b. Impose high estate or inheritance taxes
c. Impose a gift tax
d. Impose high sales taxes

62. Which government body has the least influence on foreign policy?

a. Congress
b. State Department
c. Defense Department
d. National Security Council

FCLE Practice Test #1

63. Direct democracy is used more often on which level?

a. National
b. State
c. Local
d. Supranational

64. What is the main purpose of the census?

a. To monitor illegal immigration
b. To apportion seats in the House of Representatives
c. To help determine federal income tax rates
d. To reapportion seats in the United States Senate

65. In 1937, President Franklin D. Roosevelt was accused by opponents of trying to "pack the court," and his plan for courts was defeated by the US Senate. What was Roosevelt's plan for the judicial branch at that time?

a. Roosevelt wanted only Democrats to be appointed to federal district courts
b. Roosevelt wanted only Democrats to be appointed as Supreme Court justices
c. Roosevelt wanted to raise the total number of Supreme Court justices from nine to 15
d. Roosevelt wanted to raise the total number of federal district court judges from 94 to 100

66. As a form of government, what does *oligarchy* mean?

a. Rule by one
b. Rule by a few
c. Rule by law
d. Rule by many

67. Which of the following best represents a weakness associated with the Articles of Confederation?

a. A strong national government was developed that too closely mirrored that of England.
b. The national government, not the individual state governments, had the ability to regulate trade.
c. Congress lacked the ability to tax and raise funds for governmental operation.
d. A national military was instituted, which infringed upon the rights of Americans.

68. When the Senate held an impeachment hearing against Andrew Johnson for overstepping his authority, what did they invoke?

a. Checks and balances
b. Bicameralism
c. Legislative oversight
d. Supremacy

69. The principle that freedom of speech can be limited when the exercise of that freedom creates "a clear and present danger" was established in which Supreme Court decision?

a. Plessy v. Ferguson (1896)
b. Schenck v. United States (1919)
c. Engle v. Vitale (1962)
d. Miranda v. Arizona (1966)

70. How long can members of the Federal Judiciary serve?
   a. Four years
   b. Eight years
   c. For life
   d. Six years

Refer to the following for questions 71–72:

Issues and Compromises in the United States Constitution

Issue	New Jersey Plan	Virginia Plan	Constitution
Legislative branch	A single house with members appointed by state legislatures	Two houses: Upper House with members elected by the people; Lower House elected by Upper House	Two houses: originally Senate members were elected by state legislatures, and representatives were and are still elected by the people.
Executive branch	Congress to choose an executive committee	Congress to choose a single president	President chosen by Electoral College, with electors selected by each of the states.
Judicial branch	Executive committee to appoint national judges	Congress chooses national judges	President appoints and Senate confirms Supreme Court judges.
Representation	Each state receives equal number of representatives	Representation to be based on wealth or population	Two houses created: House of Representatives based on population; Senate has two delegates from each state.

71. Which of the following conclusions can you draw on the issue of representation?
   a. Virginia's people were very poor.
   b. New Jersey started using the phrase "Liberty, Equality, and Fraternity."
   c. Virginia was probably a state with many people.
   d. Many wealthy citizens lived in New Jersey.

72. The Electoral College was created to resolve the issue of:
   a. How the wealthiest people would be represented
   b. Who would appoint the Supreme Court members
   c. How to elect senators
   d. Who would elect the chief executive

FCLE Practice Test #1

73. Which of the following was a power granted to the US Congress under the Articles of Confederation?
- a. The power to collect taxes
- b. The power to enter into treaties with foreign governments
- c. The power to enforce laws
- d. The power to regulate interstate commerce

74. Use the excerpt below from the Declaration of Independence to answer the question that follows.

> That whenever any Form of Government becomes destructive of these ends, it is the Right of the People to alter or to abolish it, and to institute new Government, laying its foundation on such principles and organizing its powers in such form, as to them shall seem most likely to effect their Safety and Happiness.

Source: National Archives and Records Administration

Which of the following principles is most directly indicated by the excerpt above?
- a. Popular sovereignty
- b. Due process
- c. Limited government
- d. Social contract theory

75. Increasing border patrols at the U.S.-Canada border was part of which legislation?
- a. USA PATRIOT Act of 2001
- b. Trade Act of 2002
- c. Protection of Lawful Commerce in Arms Act of 2005
- d. Secure Fence Act of 2006

76. Put the following events in order from oldest to most recent.
1) Martin Luther King led the March on Washington.
2) Brown v. Board of Education overturned the policy of "separate but equal" education.
3) The Student Non-Violent Coordinating Committee began staging sit-ins at segregated lunch counters in the South.
4) The arrest of Rosa Parks sparked the Montgomery Bus Boycott.
- a. 2,4,3,1
- b. 1,3,2,4
- c. 3,4,1,2
- d. 2,1,4,3

Refer to the following for question 77:

The Black Experience in America, author Norman Coombs describes a 1960s sit-in:

> "In a matter of weeks, student sit-ins were occurring at segregated lunch counters all across the South. College and high school students by the thousands joined the Civil Rights Movement. These students felt the need to form their own organization to

mobilize and facilitate the spontaneous demonstrations which were springing up everywhere."

77. Student "sit-ins" in the 1960s BEST exemplified which democratic process?

 a. Inciting fear to motivate change
 b. Litigating
 c. Lobbying
 d. Non-violent protesting

78. The Lincoln-Douglas debates resulted in

 a. the declaration of Illinois as a slave state.
 b. the split of the Democratic Party.
 c. the election of Douglas as president in 1860.
 d. the election of Lincoln to the senate in 1858.

79. Political affiliation is an example of what?

 a. Personal opinion
 b. Schema
 c. Public opinion
 d. Personal interest

80. Parks and recreation services, police and fire departments, housing services, emergency medical services, municipal courts, transportation services, and public works usually fall under the jurisdiction of which body of government?

 a. State government
 b. Federal government
 c. Federal agencies
 d. Local government

93

Answer Key and Explanations for Test #1

1. B: "...endowed by their Creator with certain unalienable Rights," is excerpted from the Declaration of Independence. These rights are unable to be taken away from individuals, referring to the colonists' rights that Great Britain could not oppress.

2. D: Madison proposed nineteen amendments to the first Congress in 1789 twelve of which were sent to the states and ten officially ratified in 1791. Neither Adams nor Jefferson was present at the Constitutional Convention.

3. A: The First Amendment addresses freedom of speech, assembly, religion, and the press. A speedy trial is covered in the Sixth Amendment, cruel and unusual punishment in the Eighth Amendment, and search and seizure in the Fourth Amendment.

4. D: Without the power of taxation, the new federal government had to rely on the states to provide the money needed to wage war against England and to pay the huge national debt accrued during the Revolution. The power to raise revenues through taxation was an essential feature of the subsequent Constitution.

5. A: Patrick Henry was not included in Morris' list of seven (Seven Who Shaped Our Destiny: The Founding Fathers as Revolutionaries, 1973). Henry, often remembered for his famous quotation "Give me liberty or give me death!" had more interest in and placed more value on state politics than national politics. He was chosen as a Virginia delegate to the Constitutional Convention, but he did not attend. Morris' list does include John Adams (b), John Jay (c), James Madison (d), and Alexander Hamilton. All of these men attended the Convention in 1776 and signed the Declaration of Independence. (In addition to attending and signing, George Washington presided over the Convention.)

6. C: Lobbyists for special interest groups petition the government. Special interest groups have been regulated because of their influence and relationships with members of Congress. PACs and special interest groups are both praised and vilified. The group Common Cause wants to end PACs.

7. C: The Federalist Party advocated a pro-British foreign policy and therefore opposed the War of 1812. This made the Federalists unpopular with many Americans; this unpopularity deepened when the war ended after several American victories. The Federalist Party did advocate a strong central government; however, this position was not a key factor in the Party's decline. This eliminates option D. Option A can be rejected because the Federalist Party did organize state political parties in states such as Connecticut, Delaware, and Maryland. Many members of the Federalist Party were pro-trade and pro-business, as many members were well-to-do businessmen. This eliminates option B.

8. C: The President must be a natural citizen, be at least 35 years old, and have lived in the US for 14 years. There is no education requirement for becoming President. Truman did not have a college education, but most Presidents have had college degrees.

9. B: Alexander Hamilton (1755/57–1804) played a pivotal role in the drafting of the Federalist Papers, a series of 85 essays designed to encourage the ratification of the US Constitution (1787). Writing under the pseudonym Publius, Alexander Hamilton, James Madison (1751–1836), and John Jay (1745–1829) addressed concerns regarding the new constitution and resulting system of governance, highlighting why a federal system of government represented the correct path forward for the United States. Although Madison and Jay (D) also contributed to the Federalist Papers, writing 29 and 5 essays respectively, Alexander Hamilton served as the primary author, with a total of 51 essays. Through his work, Hamilton focused on the need for a strong central government as well as the importance of a system of checks and balances. Hamilton's contributions helped to persuade the states to ratify the Constitution, and they continue to shape our interpretation of the Constitution today.

10. B: Shared, or concurrent, powers are those powers held by both the states and the federal government. These include taxation, borrowing money, establishing courts, and making and enforcing laws. Implied powers are those assumed by the federal government based on the "elastic clause" in Article I of the Constitution. Expressed, or enumerated, powers are those specifically granted to the federal government in Article I, Section 8 of the Constitution—e.g., the right to coin money, declare war, and regulate interstate and foreign commerce. Reserved powers are reserved exclusively to the states.

11. A: Nationalism legitimizes authority and establishes unity. Nationalism or secular nationalism influences world views and seeks to manage chaos. Secular nationalism has influenced the founding and formation of different governments throughout history.

12. B: The Founding Fathers decided that because the colonies did not have the right to elect members of Parliament, Parliament should not pass laws for them. The Declaration of Independence recognized the British Empire's government as being headed by the King of England, under whom the various local parliaments and legislative bodies served to enact laws for the peoples whom they represented. By addressing their ills to the King, the Founding Fathers sought to prevent the appearance that they acknowledged the British Parliament in London as having any authority over the American colonies.

13. B: The Supreme Court decided the case of *Montejo v. Louisiana* in 2009; therefore, this case represents the only listed decision to occur after the Cold War ended in 1991. In this case, the Supreme Court ruled that a defendant might waive the right to counsel for police interrogation, even if that interrogation was initiated after the defendant asserted that right at an arraignment or other proceeding. This decision overruled the ruling in *Michigan v. Jackson* (1986). The decision in *Gideon v. Wainwright* (A) was made in 1963, and ruled that any person charged with a serious criminal offense had the right to an attorney and to be provided one if they could not afford it. The 1964 decision in *Escobedo v. Illinois* (C) ruled that a person in police custody had the right to consult an attorney. The 1966 decision in *Miranda v. Arizona* (D) ruled that police must inform suspects of their rights to remain silent, to have a lawyer, to be appointed a lawyer if they cannot afford one, and for interrogation to stop if they invoke their right to remain silent. After this case, these rights have been commonly referred to as "Miranda rights," and arrests or interrogations wherein police do not "Mirandize" or inform suspects of these rights can be thrown out for not following procedure.

14. B: The Pilgrims' initial intention had been to settle in Northern Virginia where England had already established a presence. As there was no government in place in New England, some Pilgrims believed that they had no legal or moral duty to remain with the Pilgrims' new colony which needed their labor and support. Because of this, the Mayflower Compact created a government in New England and was signed on board the Mayflower on November 11, 1620 by each of the adult men who made the journey. The Compact's life was relatively short, due to its being superseded by the Pierce Patent in 1621 which had been signed by the king of England and had granted the Pilgrims the right of self-government in Plymouth. In spite of its short lifespan, the Mayflower Compact is credited with being North America's first constitution.

15. C: The US Supreme Court decision in *Plessy v. Ferguson* affirmed the state of Louisiana's constitutional right to offer "separate but equal" accommodations on railway lines within that state. The decision provided a legal basis for racial segregation in US society, including segregation in education and other public services. Option A can be rejected because the primary importance of the ruling was less to reinforce state's rights than to affirm the supposed legality of segregation. The decision produced increasingly significant consequences as US society continued to segregate. *Plessy v. Ferguson* did not address poll taxes or the legality of railway strikes; this eliminates options B and D.

16. C: The earliest event was the Second Continental Congress issuing the "Declaration of the Causes and Necessity for Taking up Arms" and sending the "Olive Branch Petition" to King George III, begging him to make peace with the American colonies. This took place in May of 1775. Following this, the King ignored the request for peace and approved the Prohibitory Act, declaring America to be in rebellion and thus not protected by him (D). This also took place in 1775. The next event chronologically in this list was (B). Thomas Paine published *Common Sense* in January of 1776, which urged Americans to vie immediately for independence from England. On July 4, 1776, (A) America's Second Continental Congress officially accepted the Declaration of Independence.

17. D: Implied powers in Article I, Clause 18, Section 8, the "necessary and proper" clause, give Congress the right to fund national railroad systems. Answer A is incorrect; the delegated powers did not include funding for a railroad. Nor is answer B correct because the power to support rail travel was not a denied power. This power is not expressed directly in the Constitution, so answer C is not accurate.

18. B: The versions of a bill that pass through both houses of Congress and are signed by the President must have the exact same wording. A conference committee brings the versions of the bill into alignment, but exact wording is rare.

19. A: Checks and balances prevent any branch of the government from running roughshod over the other two. Separation of powers refers to the distribution of specific powers among the three branches of government. Judicial review is the power of the courts to overturn legislative or executive acts that are deemed unconstitutional. Advice and consent is the power granted to the Senate to advise the President, ratify treaties, and confirm nominations.

20. C: Nine Vice Presidents have succeeded as President and four of them were elected President after finishing their first term.

21. D: Free public education has been a US tradition since the 18th century. State constitutions govern the educational issues of each state, although federal, state, and local governments all work together on educational issues.

22. C: Young people protested that they were old enough to fight and die for their country, yet they could not vote. Choice A is incorrect because women had the right to vote after the Nineteenth Amendment passed in 1920. Choice B is also wrong. African American males were able to vote after the Civil War. African American females gained the right in 1920. The baby boom ended in 1964. So, choice D is incorrect.

23. B: The Presidential Succession Act lists the Speaker of the House, president pro tempore of the Senate, and secretary of state next in succession after the vice president. However, anyone who succeeds as president must meet all of the legal qualifications.

Answer Key and
Explanations for Test #1

24. C: The FDIC and the SEC were both New Deal agencies created by the FDR administration in response to the stock market crash and bank failures of the Great Depression era. Both agencies still play an important role in maintaining public confidence in the nation's fundamental economic institutions.

25. C: The Anti-Federalists were a group of individuals who opposed the ratification of the US Constitution (1787). Collectively, the group argued that the Constitution created a federal government that was too strong, risking the development of tyranny. They argued that this power relegated to the federal government came at the expense of state sovereignty. Furthermore, the Anti-Federalists were concerned about the lack of a Bill of Rights, which many feared would lead to a violation of individual freedoms for the American people. Their views directly conflicted with the views of the Federalists, who supported the Constitution and the system of governance it proposed to create. The Federalists believed that the Constitution created a federal system of government that would meet the needs of the diverse American populace. Although they conceded that the Constitution did establish a strong central authority, they argued that this was necessary to manage the country in the wake of the weaknesses associated with the Articles of Confederation (1777) (A). Furthermore, the Federalists felt that the system of checks and balances instituted by the Constitution would prevent abuses of power (D). Regarding the argument of the Anti-Federalists that a lack of a bill of rights would lead to the violation of important civil liberties, the Federalists felt that the structure of government, as well as the fact that only specific powers were granted to the government, would prevent any such infringement from occurring.

26. C: Chairpersons for standing committees of Congress are chosen by leaders of the majority party.

27. D: Criminal cases are tried under both state law and federal law. The nature of the crime determines whether it is tried in state court or federal court.

28. B: A senator must be at least 30 years old, a US citizen for a minimum of nine years, and a resident of the state he represents. Every state elects two senators, and individual districts are represented in the House of Representatives.

29. C: While Civil Rights Era Supreme Court decisions did declare that segregation in schools violated the equal protection clause of the Constitution, these decisions did not lead to instantaneous desegregation of schools, as people in many locations resisted desegregation even going to the length of closing public schools to prevent it. In other areas the National Guard had to be called in to enforce orders to integrate the schools.

30. C: The decisions of the appellate court are usually final, but a decision can be reviewed en banc. This happens when a larger group of appeals judges reviews the decision.

31. C: The President is both Head of State and Chief Executive in most countries with a Presidential system. The Parliamentary system divides them into two different positions. The Head of State is often a political figurehead, and the Prime Minister serves as the Chief Executive.

32. B: The Nineteenth Amendment to the United States Constitution (1787) was ratified in 1920 and provided women with the ability to vote. The amendment states that no American can be denied the right to vote on the basis of sex. Despite the addition of the amendment to the Constitution, many women still struggled to exercise their right to fully engage in the political process. Barriers such as poll taxes, which required voters to pay a fee to vote, and literacy tests were utilized to prevent African Americans from casting their ballots. This was especially true in Southern states where Jim Crow laws were instituted to aid in discriminatory practices at various levels of political and social life. Furthermore, women from other minority groups were prevented from attaining citizenship, which limited their ability to engage in the voting process. For example, Native American women were unable to gain citizenship until 1924. This, coupled with future discriminatory practices designed to limit the voices of minority groups, limited their ability to reach full enfranchisement. These limitations continued until the passage of the Voting Rights Act of 1965, which banned the use of discriminatory practices in voting.

33. C: The President has the power to veto legislation directly or use a pocket veto by not signing a bill within ten days after receiving it. Congress adjourns during this time period. A veto can be overridden if two-thirds of the House and the two-thirds of the Senate both agree. The President must veto a complete bill and does not have the authority to veto sections or lines.

34. A: The US Constitution, Article I, Section 3 states that: "The Senate of the United States shall be composed of two Senators from each state, chosen by the legislature thereof, for six years; and each Senator shall have one vote." This was the practice until the Seventeenth Amendment was ratified on April 8, 1913. The Seventeenth Amendment states that US Senators are to be elected by the people of the states which they serve and that the state executive branches may appoint replacement Senators if a Senate seat becomes vacant mid-term, until the state legislature can arrange for a popular election.

35. C: The Northwest Ordinance of 1787 established a governmental charter for newly acquired territory northwest of the Ohio River. The ordinance guaranteed a system of republican government in new territories, detailed important civil rights for those residing there, prohibited slavery in new territories, and outlined the process by which new states would be admitted to the United States. The Northwest Ordinance is often seen as an influence on the development of the US Constitution (1787), as many of the concepts included in the Northwest Ordinance of 1787 were also included in the Constitution itself. For example, the ordinance included a detailed process by which a territory could transition to statehood, as well as qualifications that must be met to be initially eligible for the process. This admittance process was later reflected in Article IV, Section III of the US Constitution, which ensures that all new states and their citizens will have equal rights upon the state's admittance to the United States. The notion that these rights transfer equitably represented a principle essential to the expansion of the United States and allowed for the establishment and maintenance of a constitutional republic.

36. A: James Madison, John Jay, and Alexander Hamilton published *The Federalist* in the *Independent Journal* and other publications in New York. It was a response to the Anti-Federalists in New York, who were slow to ratify the Constitution because they feared it gave the central government too much authority.

37. D: Members of the House must be at least 25 years old, a US citizen for a minimum of seven years, and a resident of the state they represent. Members of the House do not necessarily need to reside in the districts they represent.

38. A: Checks and balances prevent any branch of the government from running roughshod over the other two. Separation of powers refers to the distribution of specific powers among the three branches of government. Judicial review is the power of the courts to overturn legislative or executive acts that are deemed unconstitutional. Advice and consent is the power to advise the President, ratify treaties, and confirm nominations, which is granted to the Senate in Article II of the Constitution.

39. D: The Bill of Rights was drafted by Congress to limit the authority of the government and protect the rights of individual citizens from abuse by the federal government. It was the first document to detail the rights of private citizens.

40. C: The person or group NOT instrumental in advancing civil rights and desegregation immediately after WWII was Congress. As African American soldiers came home from the war, racial discord increased. President Harry Truman appointed a Presidential Committee on Civil Rights in 1946. This committee published a report recommending that segregation and lynching be outlawed by the federal government. However, Congress ignored this report and took no action. Truman then used his presidential powers to enforce desegregation of the military and policies of "fair employment" in federal civil service jobs. The National Association for the Advancement of Colored People (NAACP) brought lawsuits against racist and discriminatory practices, and in resolving these suits, the Supreme Court further eroded segregation. For example, the Supreme Court ruled that primaries allowing only whites would be illegal, and it ended the segregation of interstate bus lines. The landmark civil rights laws were not passed by Congress until the 1960s.

41. A: The Enlightenment, also known as The Age of Enlightenment and The Age of Reason, occurred in the eighteenth century and centered on a belief in reason. The Enlightenment encouraged the ideals of liberty, self-governance, natural rights and natural law. Both the American Revolution and the French Revolution had their genesis in Enlightenment ideals which encouraged the idea that the common man should have a say in government. This was a departure from the most common types of governance, including monarchy and the belief in the divine right of kings. Enlightenment leaders tended to prefer representative republics as a form of government.

42. B: James Madison was a close friend of Thomas Jefferson and supported a stronger central government. George Mason and Robert Yates were both against expanding federal authority over the states. Benjamin Franklin was a proponent of a strong federal government, but he was from Massachusetts.

43. C: There are no formal qualifications for members of the judicial branch. However, having a background in law is an informal qualification that is considered when appointing Article III judges.

44. A: Arbitration between organizations or individuals takes place in civil court. Civil trials are similar to criminal proceedings and require a jury. Both parties, however, can agree to let a judge decide the case.

45. B: The Supreme Court ruled that statements made in interrogation are not admissible unless the defendant is informed of the right to an attorney and waives that right. The case of Miranda v. Arizona was consolidated with Westover v. United States, Vignera v. New York, and California v. Stewart.

46. B: Congress normally chooses the jurisdiction of federal courts. The Supreme Court has original jurisdiction in certain cases, which Congress cannot revoke. For example, the Supreme Court has the right to settle a dispute between states.

47. C: There are 538 electors in the Electoral College, assigned by population. There is one for each member of the congressional delegation. The District of Columbia has three electors in the Electoral College.

48. A: The Enlightenment, a 17th- to 18th-century movement centered in Europe in which philosophers focused on reason and skepticism of the church, was an important influence on the development of the United States Constitution (1787). The theories of Enlightenment philosophers such as Locke (1632–1704), Montesquieu (1689–1755), and Rousseau (1712–1778) served as guidelines for the establishment of the American system of governance and are engrained in the Constitution. Locke's focus on the protection of natural rights shaped the belief that the government must safeguard a variety of individual freedoms and ultimately served as the basis for the Bill of Rights. While Locke is recognized as a social contract theorist, Rousseau is widely credited with the establishment of the doctrine through his work *The Social Contract*. This notion that the government can only operate with the consent of the governed was a key foundational concept of the Constitution, which grants political power and establishes representation based on the will of the people. Furthermore, Montesquieu's principle of the separation of powers, the division of governmental power into three branches, influenced the structure of the American government and its organization into the judicial, executive, and legislative branches. Together, these ideals served as the basis for these and many other provisions of the US Constitution.

49. D: Benjamin Franklin primarily served as an editor of the Declaration of Independence. Thomas Hobbes wrote about the idea of a Social Contract between government and the people that was used in the Declaration of Independence as a democratic principle in his *Leviathan* (1651), describing it in the context of an authoritarian monarchy. John Locke wrote about it in his *Second Treatise of Government* (1689), describing it in the context of a liberal monarchy. Jean-Jacques Rousseau wrote about it in his *Du Contrat Social*, or *The Social Contract* (1762), in the context of a liberal republic similar to what the new USA would become. These works supplied a theoretical basis for constitutional monarchies, liberal democracies, and republicanism.

50. D: The Truman Doctrine was intended to prevent Greece and Turkey from becoming communist countries. However, its broad language had implications beyond those two nations, suggesting that US policy generally should be to aid people who resisted outside forces attempting to impose communist rule. This doctrine led to US involvement in Korea and Vietnam, where US forces fought against communist forces in those nations. The United States did have a plan for assisting the European economies, but it was the Marshall Plan, not the Truman Doctrine. This eliminates choice B. While President Truman did establish a President's Committee on Civil Rights, it was not as a result of the Truman Doctrine. This eliminates answer A. Finally, when inflation plagued the postwar US economy, the federal government took measures to address inflation and other economic issues, rather than steering clear of them. This eliminates choice C.

51. A: The Age of Enlightenment was a time of scientific and philosophical achievement. Also called the Age of Reason, it was a time when human thought and reason were prized.

52. D: It is the duty of the President to see that federal laws are enforced. National laws are not subject to state laws or interpretations in matters constitutionally delegated to the federal government. Choice A is incorrect, as the governor of a state does have power; he cannot act, however, in defiance of constitutional federal law. Choice B is incorrect as well, as the conflict in Vietnam had nothing to do with the situation in Arkansas. Choice C is incorrect, as the Constitution outlines powers delegated to both levels of government, with regard to different spheres of influence.

53. A: The Sherman Antitrust Act outlawed "every contract, combination ... or conspiracy in restraint of trade or commerce among the several States, or with foreign nations." Option C describes trade within states; because the Sherman Antitrust Act does not address such trade, option C can be rejected. Options B and D each describe a use of the Sherman Antitrust Act; i.e., the Act was instrumental in breaking up both the Standard Oil trust and the AT&T monopoly. However, neither of these particular uses are as influential as the general outlawing of acts restraining trade

between states; rather, it was the general prohibition which made these particular applications (and others) possible. This eliminates options B and D.

54. C: Massachusetts did set a valuable example for other states by stipulating that its constitution should be created via a special convention rather than via the legislature. This way, the constitution would take precedence over the legislature, which would be subject to the rules of the constitution. It is not true that twelve states had new constitutions by the end of 1777. By this time, ten of the states had new constitutions. It is not true that Connecticut and Massachusetts retained their colonial charters minus the British parts. Connecticut and Rhode Island were the states that preserved their colonial charters. They simply removed any parts referring to British rule. Massachusetts did not formalize its new constitution in 1778. This state did not actually finish the process of adopting its new constitution until 1780.

55. B: Due process refers to the right of a defendant to confront accusers and to provide a defense.

56. D: The war ended during Nixon's administration, not during LBJ's term. The Great Society program included legislation to create Medicare (A), eliminate obstacles hindering the right to vote (B), provide federal funding for education (C), and establish the Department of Housing and Urban Development (HUD). The Great Society also included a number of programs aimed at alleviating poverty. Johnson's social reform accomplishments were overshadowed by the Vietnam War during his last two years in office.

57. D: The Massachusetts Constitution was drafted in 1780 by John Adams (1735–1826) and includes a preamble, declaration of rights, description of the principles and framework of government, and amendments. The document served as a model for the development of the United States Constitution (1787) in both its structure and contents. The section of text above is from Article I of the Massachusetts Declaration of Rights, which collectively outlines the individual rights and freedoms of the citizens of Massachusetts. In general, the Massachusetts Declaration of Rights helped shape the philosophical foundation of the US Bill of Rights through its inclusion of protections such as due process and private property. Upon ratification of the Bill of Rights, the US Constitution incorporated such protections to ensure that the government did not infringe upon the rights of its people. The United States Constitution is organized into a series of articles, each of which pertain to a different aspect of governmental operations. For example, Article I (A) established the Legislative Branch of the US government, detailed its structures and duties, and provided it with the power to make laws. Articles II and III serve a similar purpose, with Article II (B) focused on the powers and duties of the Executive Branch and the President of the United States, and Article III (C) dedicated to the establishment of an independent judicial branch.

58. C: The male passengers of the Mayflower signed the Compact after a disagreement regarding where in the Americas they should establish a colony. The Compact served as a written basis for laws in their subsequent colony. Because the Mayflower Compact did not list particular rights, it is not best understood as a blueprint for the Bill of Rights. This eliminates choice B. Though the Compact did in part serve as a basis for government, it did not declare independence from King James; its last line, for example, specifically refers to King James as the writers' sovereign. This eliminates choice A. Finally, although the Mayflower Compact does include religious language, it is a brief document that does not detail, defend, or establish as official any particular religious doctrine, including Puritan religious doctrine. This eliminates choice D.

59. B: The term "Manifest Destiny" originated with the annexation of Texas as Americans began to envision a nation that spread from coast to coast. Texas entered the union as a slave state. The Monroe Doctrine addressed European intervention in the Western Hemisphere, which was not an issue in the annexation of Texas. Mexican resentment of the annexation was a factor in the Mexican War, which began the following year.

60. C: The US Supreme Court justices had decided that *Brown* would have a unanimous holding (the legal term for a court's rulings or decisions) before they determined what that holding would be, which resulted in a fairly narrow holding that "the plaintiffs and others similarly situated for whom the actions have been brought are, by reason of the segregation complained of, deprived of the equal protection of the laws guaranteed by the Fourteenth Amendment." This decision was used in later Civil Rights cases as a legal precedent for the idea that the doctrine of "separate but equal" was inherently unconstitutional, reversing the precedent set by *Plessy v. Ferguson*.

61. D: Proponents of legislating greater societal income equity support imposing a progressive income tax, which taxes the wealthy at a higher rate; an inheritance tax, which prevents the wealthy from passing all their wealth on to the next generation; and a gift tax, which prevents the wealthy from simply giving their wealth away.

62. A: Although Congress must agree to pay for foreign policy dictated by the president, it does not decide foreign policy.

63. C: Direct democracy is the right of every citizen to attend meetings and vote on issues. A simple majority vote wins in a direct democracy. The logistics for direct democracy, such as holding a meeting for all state citizens, make it difficult for state and national governments to institute. Direct democracy is used on a local level in small New England towns.

64. B: Article I of the Constitution mandates the taking of a census every ten years. The purpose was to be sure that each state was proportionately represented in Congress according to its population as specified in the Constitution. Census data is also used to allocate federal funding for various programs and for shaping economic policies. Individual data collected by the US Bureau of the Census is kept confidential for seventy-two years and does not affect income tax rates. Every state has two seats in the Senate regardless of population.

65. C: President Roosevelt's plan for the judicial branch in 1937 was to raise the total number of Supreme Court justices from 9 to 15. His plan was defeated by the US Senate. The other answer choices sound like plausible ways that one might try to "pack the courts," but they are not correct answers for that time period, which students with a general history knowledge at this grade level should know.

66. B: Oligarchy is defined as the rule by few. An example is aristocracy, which in ancient Greece, was government by an elite group of citizens as opposed to a monarchy. In later times, it meant government by the class of aristocrats, a privileged group, as opposed to democracy. The rule of one is called autocracy. Examples include monarchy, dictatorship, and many others. The rule by law is called a republic. Some examples are constitutional republics, parliamentary republics, and federal republics. The rule by many could apply to democracy, which governs according to the people's votes, or to the collective leadership form of socialism, where no one individual has too much power.

67. C: The Articles of Confederation (1777) served as the first governing document of the United States and was created to unify the 13 American colonies as they fought against England in the Revolutionary War (1775–1783). Americans feared the establishment of a strong central authority that would be similar to the tyranny of the British monarchy. Consequently, they sought to establish a weak central government (A) through the Articles of Confederation in which individual states maintained a great deal of power and overall sovereignty. Although effective in helping the United

States maintain governance throughout the American Revolution, the Articles of Confederation had many weaknesses. The central government had no power to tax, instead relying on voluntary contributions by the states that were typically inadequate in meeting the needs of the country. Additionally, as a result of the fears stemming from the power of the British Crown, no executive branch was established to enforce laws. There was also no judicial branch at the national level, rendering the national government incapable of mitigating disputes among the states. Furthermore, changes or amendments to the Articles required the unanimous consent of all states, making modifications to the document very challenging. The central government also lacked the ability to regulate trade (B) or establish a national military (D). These weaknesses led to the need to establish a new system of governance under the United States Constitution (1787).

68. A: Checks and balances were established to keep one branch of government from taking too much authority. When Johnson violated the Tenure of Office Act by replacing Secretary of War Edwin Stanton, Johnson was impeached, but the final vote in the Senate trial came up one vote short of the number needed to convict him.

69. B: Charles Schenck was arrested for distributing leaflets advocating opposition to the draft during World War I. The Supreme Court unanimously decided that free speech could be restricted if it creates "a clear and present danger." This ruling was subsequently modified by Brandenburg v. Ohio in 1969. Plessy supported the "separate but equal" doctrine; Engle ruled that school prayer was unconstitutional; Miranda required police to advise criminal suspects of their rights.

70. C: Article III judges are appointed for life and can retire at 65. They can only be removed from their posts by impeachment in the House and conviction in the Senate. Having judges serve life terms is meant to allow them to serve without being governed by the changing opinions of the public.

71. C: Virginia's plan called for representation based on population. So, that plan would help states with larger populations. Choice A is incorrect because Virginia would not want representation based on wealth if it were a poor state. Choice B uses the motto of the French Revolution. So, this has nothing to do with the US Constitution. Choice D is incorrect because the New Jersey Plan did not ask for representation to be based on wealth.

72. D: The Electoral College was a compromise for a way to elect the president. Choice A is incorrect because wealth has nothing to do with the role of the Electoral College. Choice B is wrong as well. The appointment of Supreme Court justices is not part of the Electoral College. That is a job for the chief executive. Electing senators is also not the responsibility of the Electoral College. So, this makes choice C incorrect.

73. B: The Articles of Confederation granted the federal Congress the power to enter into treaties. It did not grant Congress the abilities to collect taxes, enforce laws or to regulate interstate commerce (it could impose some regulations on commerce with foreign entities), these shortcomings led to the eventual abandonment of the Articles of Confederation in favor of the Constitution, which is still in force today.

74. D: Social contract theory is a well-known Enlightenment (1685–1815) theory that heavily influenced many of the foundational documents of the United States government. Philosophers such as John Locke (1632–1704) articulated the notion that governments exist for the purpose of protecting the natural rights of their citizens. In accordance with this social contract, and in exchange for protection of these rights, citizens agree to abide by regulations established by the government. Locke theorized that if a government failed to protect its citizens' rights, or if it behaved in an abusive manner, the citizenry had the right and responsibility to overthrow the regime. The excerpt above from the Declaration of Independence (1776) reiterates this aspect of social contract theory, stating that the people have the right to abolish a system of government that fails to protect their rights and to replace it with a new system of governance. The content of the text is related to the principle of popular sovereignty (A) in its assertion that the people hold the power behind government; however, the excerpt focuses on the idea that the people have the right to abolish the government if it fails to protect their rights, a notion which aligns more closely with the principle of social contract theory. Neither the philosophy of due process (B) nor that of limited government (C) directly relate to the content of the text above. Due process describes the idea that the government must take certain steps to infringe upon the rights or liberty of individuals. Limited government is a system in which the power of the government is contained through legal doctrine.

75. A: Increasing border controls on the Canada-U.S. border was part of the USA PATRIOT Act of 2001 and affected the private and public sectors of people traveling between those two countries. The other choices sound like they could be related to events between the U.S. and Canada. For example, lawful commerce in arms could relate to guns sold between countries, but it was for guns within the United States. So, choice C is incorrect. Choice B is wrong because a Trade Act might apply to U.S.-Canada trade, but not to border patrols. Choice D is wrong because the "Fence" Act applied to the Mexico-U.S. border, not the Canada-U.S. border.

76. A: Brown v. Board of Education was decided in 1954. Rosa Parks was arrested in 1955. The lunch counter sit-ins were staged in 1960. The March on Washington took place in 1963.

77. D: Student sit-ins were an example in the 1960s of non-violent protesting that took place mostly under the guidance and philosophy of Martin Luther King, Jr. These were not displays of Black Power to incite fear, although those also occurred separately in the 1960s under leaders such as Malcolm X. Sit-ins were not a form of lobbying or litigation, although those are also non-violent in their nature.

78. B: The debates between Lincoln, a Republican, and Douglas, a Democrat, resulted in Douglas making statements about slavery that the South would not accept. This resulted in the split of the Democratic Party and the defeat of Douglas in the presidential election in 1860.

79. B: A schema is a belief system that uses personal experiences, socialization, background, and ideological convictions to interpret a subject. A person's political affiliation is an example of a schema.

80. D: Local governments are usually divided into counties and municipalities. Municipalities oversee parks and recreation services, police and fire departments, housing services, emergency medical services, municipal courts, transportation services, and public works.

FCLE Practice Test #2

1. The president serves as commander-in-chief. What are the president's two limitations in that role?

  a. The president cannot declare war or oversee military regulations.
  b. The president cannot enforce blockades or declare war.
  c. The president cannot enforce quarantines or oversee military regulations.
  d. The president cannot enforce blockades or quarantines.

Refer to the following for question 2:

Voter Issue from 2008:

ISSUE 3: PROPOSED CONSTITUTIONAL AMENDMENT TO AMEND THE CONSTITUTION TO PROTECT PRIVATE PROPERTY RIGHTS IN GROUND WATER, LAKES AND OTHER WATERCOURSES (Proposed by Joint Resolution of the General Assembly of Ohio) To adopt Section 19b of Article I of the Constitution of the State of Ohio A YES vote means approval of the amendment. A NO vote means disapproval of the amendment. A majority YES vote is required for the amendment to be adopted. If approved, this amendment shall take effect December 1, 2008.

League Explanation of Issue 3: This proposed amendment resulted from the Ohio legislature's passage of the Great Lakes Water Compact this past spring. Some lawmakers feared final approval of the Compact might limit private water rights. The constitutional amendment is intended to recognize that:

- Property owners have a protected right to the "reasonable use" of the ground water flowing under their property and of the water in a lake or watercourse that is on or flows through their property.
- An owner has the right to give or sell these interests to a governmental body.
- The public welfare supersedes individual property owners' rights. The state and political subdivisions may regulate such waters to the extent state law allows.
- The proposed amendment would not affect public use of Lake Erie and the state's other navigable waters.
- The rights confirmed by this amendment may not be limited by sections of the Ohio Constitution addressing home rule, public debt and public works, conservation of natural resources, and the prohibition of the use of "initiative" and "referendum" on property taxes.

2. Which of the following conclusions is correct?

  a. The state of Ohio will give up rights to the control of Lake Erie in favor of public rights.
  b. People who own property with water on it cannot sell that land to the state.
  c. The state considers the public's welfare to be more important than an individual property owner's rights.
  d. This issue was created without input from any lawmakers or organizations.

3. What judicial system did America borrow from England?

   a. Due process
   b. Federal law
   c. Commerce law
   d. Common law

4. After the Civil War, President Andrew Johnson disagreed with Congress over Reconstruction policies. Which action by President Johnson best describes the grounds for which he was impeached?

   a. He dismissed a Cabinet member without congressional permission.
   b. He refused to enforce the Fourteenth Amendment.
   c. He sought to disenfranchise former Confederate officers.
   d. He violated Constitution law in forming a third political party.

5. Which of the following is a power held only by the federal government?

   a. The power to levy taxes, borrow money, and spend money
   b. The power to award copyrights and patents to people or groups
   c. The power to establish the criteria that qualify a person to vote
   d. The power to ratify proposed amendments to the Constitution

6. Which of the following is NOT an example of a shared, or concurrent, power?

   a. The power to build roads
   b. The power to coin money
   c. The power to collect taxes
   d. The power to establish courts

7. Reference the excerpt below from Federalist No 51 to answer the question that follows.

> To what expedient, then, shall we finally resort, for maintaining in practice the necessary partition of power among the several departments, as laid down in the Constitution? The only answer that can be given is, that as all these exterior provisions are found to be inadequate, the defect must be supplied, by so contriving the interior structure of the government as that its several constituent parts may, by their mutual relations, be the means of keeping each other in their proper places.

Source: National Archives and Records Administration

The text included above best supports which of the following arguments presented in Federalist No 51 regarding the US Constitution?

   a. Each of the three branches of government will naturally exert only the power explicitly granted to it.
   b. The President's cabinet will serve as the heads of various governmental departments in the new government.
   c. Power in the new government will be evenly divided between each branch of government.
   d. A system of checks and balances will prevent any one branch of government from gaining too much power.

8. What was the purpose of the Sherman Anti-Trust Act?

a. To prevent unions from striking
b. To prevent restraints on free trade
c. To encourage international trade
d. To prevent corporate tax evasion

9. Describe the influence of Brutus I on the development of the US system of governance.

a. It promoted the separation of powers between the three branches of government.
b. It led to the development of a strong central government.
c. It encouraged the addition of the Bill of Rights to the US Constitution.
d. It argued for the incorporation of a strong central judiciary.

10. In 1777, the United States Congress adopted the Articles of Confederation. The Articles of Confederation limited the power of the federal government by denying it:

a. The power to borrow money
b. The power to declare war
c. The power to make international treaties
d. The power to raise taxes

11. Which of the following BEST describes the significance of the US Supreme Court's decision in the Dred Scott case?

a. The ruling effectively declared slavery to be a violation of the Constitution.
b. The ruling guaranteed full citizenship rights to freed slaves.
c. The ruling turned many Southerners against the Supreme Court.
d. The ruling furthered the gap between North and South and hastened the Civil War.

12. Which of these factors was NOT a direct contributor to the beginning of the American Revolution?

a. The attitudes of American colonists toward Great Britain following the French and Indian War
b. The attitudes of leaders in Great Britain toward the American colonies and imperialism
c. James Otis's court argument against Great Britain's Writs of Assistance as breaking natural law
d. Lord Grenville's Proclamation of 1763, the Sugar Act, the Currency Act, and especially the Stamp Act

13. Public policy is developed at what level?

a. State level
b. Local level
c. Federal level
d. All of the above

14. Thomas Jefferson embraced a theological philosophy called deism, which promotes which of the following?

a. Abolition
b. Atheism
c. Separation of church and state
d. A theocratic central government

FCLE Practice Test #2

15. **Which of the following was a contemporary argument against The Bill of Rights?**
    a. The concern that it didn't apply to the states.
    b. The belief that a bill of rights would infringe upon states' rights.
    c. The concern that specifically stating one right would create an argument against an unstated right.
    d. The belief that the Bill of Rights would be too great a check on government's ability to function.

16. **Who negotiates treaties?**
    a. The President
    b. The House of Representatives
    c. Ambassadors
    d. The Senate

17. **Which of the following US Constitutional Amendments lowered the voting age to eighteen?**
    a. The 24th
    b. The 25th
    c. The 26th
    d. The 27th

18. **With the end of Reconstruction in 1877, which of the following was true regarding African Americans in the South?**
    a. They soon took control of state legislatures
    b. They formed a new political party to protect their own interests
    c. They were able to rise quickly into the economic middle class
    d. They were kept from voting by poll taxes and literacy tests

Refer to the following for question 19:

Chart—Percentage of African Americans in Certain Military Ranks, 1964-1966

Rank E-6 (Staff Sergeant or Petty Officer, First Class)

	1964	1965	1966
Army	13.9	15.5	18.1
Navy	4.7	5.0	5.6
Marine Corps	5.0	5.3	10.4

Source: Office, Deputy Assistant Secretary of Defense (Civil Rights)

19. In the early 1960s, President Kennedy became more committed to helping civil rights causes, including the cause of desegregation in the military. Based on this chart, what conclusion about African Americans in 1964-66 military ranks can be made?

a. African Americans started making up a larger percentage of Major or Lieutenant Commander Ranks in the Army, Navy, and Marines.

b. African Americans started making up a larger percentage of Staff Sergeant or Petty Officer Ranks in the Army, Navy, and Marines.

c. African Americans started making up a larger percentage of Staff Sergeant or Petty Officer Ranks in the Army and Marines, but not in the Navy.

d. The percentage of African-American Staff Sergeants or Petty Officers grew between 1964 and 1965 but then declined again between 1965 and 1966.

20. Which court case established the Court's ability to overturn laws that violated the Constitution?

a. *Miranda v. Arizona*
b. *Marbury v. Madison*
c. *United States v. Curtiss-Wright Export Corporation*
d. *Brown v. Board of Education of Topeka*

21. How are members of the Federal Judiciary chosen?

a. They are elected by voters.
b. They are appointed by the president and confirmed by the House of Representatives.
c. They are chosen by a committee.
d. They are appointed by the president and confirmed by the Senate.

22. The 1783 Treaty of Paris included which of the following agreements?

a. Boundaries were established for the United States, including the southern tip of Florida as the southernmost boundary.

b. Britain was allowed to keep both Canada and Florida as imperial British territories under the terms of the Treaty of Paris.

c. The treaty stipulated that all private creditors in Britain were prohibited from making future debt collections from Americans.

d. Britain and the other most powerful countries of Europe recognized the United States' independence as a nation.

23. Which of the following ideas was present in the Declaration of Independence and served as an important influence on future movements designed to protect minority groups?

a. The commitment to the establishment of political parties to curb the impact of factions
b. The notion that government attains its power from the consent of the governed
c. The focus on the prevention of tyrannical rule that would infringe on the rights of the people
d. The argument that all men are created equal and have certain unalienable rights

24. Which of the following examples is protected as an expression of free speech?

    a. Draftees of the Vietnam War who burned their draft cards

    b. A radio personality who states on air that the President should be shot over his most recent budget proposal

    c. Pro-life protesters who carry "wanted" signs displaying the photos and home/work addresses of abortion providers during a legally sanctioned protest

    d. A high school teacher who allows her students to use profanity when creating poetry

25. Which line of the chart below best lists the kinds of cases over which the US federal court system has jurisdiction?

Jurisdiction of the Federal Court System

Line 1	Constitutional law	Bankruptcy	Most contract cases
Line 2	Constitutional law	Most contract cases	Most criminal cases
Line 3	Constitutional law	Bankruptcy	Disputes between states
Line 4	Constitutional law	Most personal injury cases	Disputes between states

    a. Line 1

    b. Line 2

    c. Line 3

    d. Line 4

26. Which US Founding Father is credited with founding the Federalist Party?

    a. John Adams

    b. Thomas Jefferson

    c. Alexander Hamilton

    d. George Washington

27. Which of the following is NOT true about democracy and the formation of the United States?

    a. The founding fathers stated in the Constitution that the United States would be a democracy.

    b. The Declaration of Independence did not dictate democracy but stated its principles.

    c. The United States Constitution stipulated that government be elected by the people.

    d. The United States Constitution had terms to protect some, but not all, of the people.

28. Among landmark Supreme Court civil rights cases from Oklahoma, which of these occurred the most recently?

    a. In *Guinn v. United States,* the Supreme Court struck down a grandfather clause exempting white voters from a required literacy test.

    b. In *Lane v. Wilson,* the Supreme Court struck down a state law that racially manipulated voting by putting a time limit on registration.

    c. In *Sipuel v. Board of Regents of University of Oklahoma,* the Supreme Court required Oklahoma to admit a black woman into law school.

    d. In *McLaurin v. Oklahoma State Regents,* the Supreme Court set the precedent with higher education for *Brown v. Board of Education.*

29. What is the term for the general agreement on fundamental principles of governance and the values supporting them?

    a. Rule of law
    b. Nationalism
    c. Political culture
    d. Democratic consensus

30. "Old enough to fight, old enough to vote" became a slogan for a youth voting rights movement after the World War II military draft age was lowered to 18, while 21 remained the minimum voting age. The Vietnam War draft brought more urgency to the youth voting rights movement and resulted in which amendment to lower the voting age to 18?

    a. 24th Amendment
    b. 25th Amendment
    c. 26th Amendment
    d. 27th Amendment

31. Thomas Paine's *Common Sense* influenced which American document that ultimately helped shape the Constitution?

    a. The Articles of Confederation
    b. The Declaration of Independence
    c. The Bill of Rights
    d. The Treaty of Greenville

32. Texas slaves were emancipated on which of the following occasions:

    a. As a consequence of the 1836 agreements granting independence to the Republic of Texas
    b. As part of the 1848 Treaty of Guadalupe-Hidalgo that ended the Mexican American War
    c. As a result of Lincoln's 1863 Emancipation Proclamation that freed slaves in the Confederacy
    d. As a ramification of the Union's occupation of Texas in 1865

33. Every citizen 18 years of age and older has the constitutional right to vote. What do states govern in the voting process?

    a. The registration for and timing of federal elections
    b. The administration and timing of federal elections
    c. The registration for and administration of federal elections
    d. The registration for federal elections only

34. The Seneca Falls Convention of 1848 marked the beginning of which of the following?

    a. Abolitionist movement
    b. Republican Party
    c. Temperance movement
    d. Women's rights movement

35. The civil rights act that outlawed segregation in schools and public places also did which of the following?

    a. Gave minorities the right to vote
    b. Established women's right to vote
    c. Outlawed unequal voter registration
    d. Provided protection for children

36. Which of the following is NOT correct concerning the Articles of Confederation?

    a. They established the confederation's name as The United States of America.

    b. They gave one vote apiece to each state in the Congress of the Confederation.

    c. They established the freedom, sovereignty, and equality of individual states.

    d. They gave individual states the sovereign right to wage war using state militias.

37. In the Constitution of the United States, which of the following powers is reserved for the states?

    a. Taxation

    b. Declaring war

    c. Regulation of intrastate trade

    d. Granting patents and copyrights

38. In writing the sole dissenting opinion in a famous Supreme Court case, Justice John Marshall Harlan wrote these words:

> Our Constitution is color-blind, and neither knows nor tolerates classes among citizens. In respect of civil rights, all citizens are equal before the law.

What was the case about which he was writing?

    a. Marbury v. Madison

    b. Plessy v. Ferguson

    c. Gideon v. Wainwright

    d. Brown v. Board of Education

39. Civic responsibility differs from personal responsibility in that the subject matter of civic responsibility is mainly which of the following?

    a. Fair reporting of government actions

    b. Fair dealings between governments

    c. A person's responsibilities as a citizen

    d. A person's responsibilities as a government worker

40. How did the ruling in *Marbury v. Madison* alter the Supreme Court's power in the federal government?

    a. It lessened it. The Supreme Court was concerned about the possibility of judges overturning laws enacted by voters through referendums and took away that power.

    b. It increased it. The decision in *Marbury v. Madison* gave the Supreme Court its now traditional right to overturn legislation.

    c. It increased it. The decision in *Marbury v. Madison* strengthened the Supreme Court's Constitutional right to overturn legislation.

    d. There was no change. *Marbury v. Madison* was a case involving a president who was unwilling to obey laws enacted by his predecessor; there was nothing about the case or decision that would have more than a cursory connection to federal powers of government

41. The word democracy comes from two Greek root words meaning what?

    a. People and rule

    b. People and vote

    c. City and state

    d. Tyrant and overthrow

42. The constitutional rights of citizens are protected in what?

a. Bicameral legislature
b. Authoritarian regimes
c. Constitutional republics
d. Pure democracies

43. Of the following landmark US Supreme Court decisions, which one addressed the regulation of interstate navigation?

a. *Gibbons v. Ogden* (1824)
b. *Ableman v. Booth* (1859)
c. *Plessy v. Ferguson* (1896)
d. *The Paquete Habana* (1900)

44. What does the 10th Amendment establish?

a. Any power not given to the federal government belongs to the states or the people.
b. The president is responsible for executing and enforcing laws created by Congress.
c. Congress has the authority to declare war.
d. The Supreme Court has the authority to interpret the Constitution.

45. Use the excerpt below from the Fifth Amendment of the United States Constitution to answer the question that follows.

> No person shall be held to answer for a capital, or otherwise infamous crime, unless on a presentment or indictment of a Grand Jury, except in cases arising in the land or naval forces, or in the Militia, when in actual service in time of War or public danger; nor shall any person be subject for the same offence to be twice put in jeopardy of life or limb; nor shall be compelled in any criminal case to be a witness against himself, nor be deprived of life, liberty, or property, without due process of law.

Source: National Archives and Records Administration

Which of the following documents may have served as an inspiration for the text included above?

a. The Magna Carta
b. The Anti-Federalist Papers
c. The Northwest Ordinances
d. The Mayflower Compact

46. Thomas Jefferson is the primary author of which of the following documents?

a. Federalist No 10
b. The Declaration of Independence
c. The United States Constitution
d. Articles of Confederation

47. The House Committee on Oversight and Government Reform oversees and reforms government operations. Which Senate committee works with that committee?

a. Senate Committee on Banking, Housing, and Urban Affairs
b. Senate Committee on Homeland Security and Government Affairs
c. Senate Committee on Rules and Administration
d. Senate Appropriations Committee

48. The concept of checks and balances is evident in which of the following?
a. Federal judiciary appeals
b. Presidential veto
c. States' rights
d. The House and the Senate

49. The president may serve a maximum of _____ according to the ___ Amendment.
a. Three four-year terms; 23rd
b. Two four-year terms; 22nd
c. One four-year term; 22nd
d. Two four-year terms; 23rd

50. The 1887 General Allotment Act, also known as the Dawes Act, had a policy of giving private property ownership to Native Americans in order to divide the Native American reservations into individual "family farms." What was a practical result of this policy?
a. Many Native American tribes lost large portions of their reservations.
b. Many Native Americans became assimilated to the American culture of family farming.
c. The Nez Perce Conflict occurred between Nez Perce Native Americans and US army forces.
d. American settlers moved to lands formerly owned by Native Americans and slaughtered most of the buffalo that Native Americans depended on for their livelihood.

51. The US government is best understood as a federalist government because:
a. The legislative branch consists of two representative bodies.
b. It is a representative democracy rather than a direct democracy.
c. Political power is divided between the federal government and the states.
d. A national Constitution shapes national legislation.

52. In the Progressive Era of the late 1890s and early 1900s, political reformers wanted to make sure government represented the peoples' will. An "initiative" process began in 1898 in South Dakota and then spread to other states. Which definition BEST describes the initiative process?
a. It allowed voting citizens to give their judgment on proposed legislation before state legislators voted on the same legislation.
b. It allowed voters to gather petitions demanding special elections when they wanted to recall an unpopular public official, thereby allowing them to "un-elect" that official.
c. It allowed citizens to introduce legislation proposals at a local or state level by gathering petitions, and proposals would then be addressed by lawmakers or placed on ballots for a vote.
d. It allowed citizens to visit state legislatures and give testimony supporting a certain issue, thereby encouraging the state lawmakers to propose and pass legislation on that same issue.

53. During the Civil Rights era of the 1950s, which of the following events furthered the civil rights cause?
a. The Supreme Court's decision in *Brown v. Board of Education of Topeka*
b. Governor Orval Faubus' actions relative to Little Rock High School
c. Eisenhower's use of the 101st Airborne Division to protect students
d. Both A and C

54. The Seventeenth Amendment to the US Constitution made the US government more democratic in which of the following ways?

a. By requiring state governors to be selected by popular election rather than by state electoral colleges

b. By mandating a regular national census to reevaluate state representation in the House of Representatives

c. By requiring US senators to be selected by popular election rather than by state legislatures

d. By mandating regular state censuses to determine appropriate representation in state Houses of Representatives

Refer to the following for question 55:

Mother Jones, who was a labor activist, wrote the following about children working in cotton mills in Alabama: "Little girls and boys, barefooted, walked up and down between the endless rows of spindles, reaching thin little hands into the machinery to repair snapped threads. They crawled under machinery to oil it. They replaced spindles all day long; all night through…six-year-olds with faces of sixty did an eight-hour shift for ten cents a day; the machines, built in the North, were built low for the hands of little children."

55. Which of the following do you think happened after this was published?

a. More children signed up to work in the factories.

b. Cotton factories in the South closed.

c. Laws were passed to prevent child labor.

d. The pay scale for these children was increased.

56. The primary claim in Federalist No 31 is most closely tied to which section of the US Constitution?

a. Article I, Section 8, which grants Congress the right to tax

b. The Bill of Rights, which details the protection of civil liberties

c. Article V, which outlines the process for amending the Constitution

d. Article VI, Clause 2, which describes the supremacy of the federal government over state governments

57. One reason the Articles of Confederation created a weak government was because it limited Congress's ability to do what?

a. Declare war

b. Conduct a census

c. Vote

d. Tax

58. Which of the following best describes the impact of the Mayflower Compact on the development of American government?

a. It established the framework for a federal system of government between the colonies and the British monarchy.

b. It introduced the concept of a social contract in which the colonists established a government based on the consent of the governed.

c. It promoted the development of direct democracy in which each male had the ability to engage in the political process.

d. It instituted a system where colonial leadership was based upon heredity prior to the transition to democratic rule.

59. Article III judges who can retire but still try cases on a full-time or part-time basis are called _____.

    a. Recalled judges
    b. Senior judges
    c. Chief judges
    d. Elder judges

60. Which of the following was a stated reason for Jefferson's opposition to the Bank of the United States?

    a. He did not think the Bank would effectively further his goal of establishing a strong central government.
    b. He was a strict constructionist.
    c. He believed the Bank would give an unfair advantage to the southern states.
    d. He distrusted the fiscal policies of the Democratic-Republicans.

61. What do the American labor union movement, the antislavery movement, the women's suffrage movement, and the civil rights movement all have in common?

    a. They all used political protest.
    b. They all appealed to legal precedent.
    c. They all came from political homogeneity.
    d. They were all protected by the commerce clause.

62. Which of the following best details the impact of Thomas Paine's *Common Sense* on the Declaration of Independence?

    a. It detailed the importance of a system of checks and balances.
    b. It highlighted the need for an independent judiciary.
    c. It reiterated the significance of rejecting hereditary rule and the monarchy.
    d. It introduced the idea of a federal system of government.

63. What was representative democracy likely motivated by?

    a. An increase in population
    b. Aristocracy
    c. The Supreme Court
    d. States passing laws that violated federal laws

64. A law proposed in Congress but not yet passed is called:

    a. A bill
    b. A proposal
    c. An introduced law
    d. A debate

65. How is a tie broken in the Senate?

    a. The president pro tempore casts the deciding vote.
    b. The Speaker of the House votes.
    c. They vote again.
    d. The vice president votes.

66. The Office of Management and Budget helps the President prepare the federal budget. What is it a part of?

a. United States Trade Agency
b. Federal Reserve Board
c. Securities and Exchange Commission
d. Executive Office of the President

67. How is a tie in the Electoral College broken to choose the President?

a. Each state's delegation in the House of Representatives gets a vote, and the majority wins
b. Each state's delegation in the Senate gets a vote, and the majority wins
c. The former Vice President becomes President
d. The Speaker of the House casts the deciding vote

Refer to the following for question 68:

> "As you know, I will soon be visiting the People's Republic of China and the Soviet Union. I go there with no illusions. We have great differences with both powers. We shall continue to have great differences. But peace depends on the ability of great powers to live together on the same planet despite their differences."

68. Which president gave this speech, as he was about to become the first US President to visit the communist People's Republic of China?

a. President John F. Kennedy
b. President Lyndon B. Johnson
c. President Richard M. Nixon
d. President Gerald R. Ford

69. Which of the following statements is NOT true regarding the Tea Act of 1773?

a. The British East India Company was suffering financially because Americans were buying tea smuggled from Holland.
b. Parliament granted concessions to the British East India Company to ship tea straight to America, bypassing England.
c. Colonists found that even with added taxes, tea directly shipped by the British East India Company cost less, and they bought it.
d. American colonists refused to buy less expensive tea from the British East India Company on the principle of taxation.

70. Which of the following accurately describes the process by which government officials may be impeached and removed from office?

a. Charges are brought by the House of Representatives and tried in the Senate.
b. Charges are brought by the Senate and tried in the House of Representatives.
c. Charges are brought by the Attorney-General and tried in Congress.
d. Charges are brought by both houses of Congress and tried in the Supreme Court.

71. What were the Federalist Papers meant to accomplish?

a. To encourage people to join the Federalist Party
b. To explain the necessity of the federalist system
c. To assist in the ratification of the Constitution
d. To expose a series of scandals relating to the Federalist Party

117

72. Modern separation of powers preserves which principle?

a. Mixed government
b. Democracy
c. Parliamentary system
d. Presidential system

73. Which government system vests almost all control in a central government?

a. Federation
b. Democracy
c. Unitary system
d. Confederation

74. The votes of how many states were needed to ratify the Constitution?

a. Five
b. Ten
c. Nine
d. Seven

75. How can Congress override the presidential veto of a bill?

a. By a majority vote in the House and a two-thirds majority in the Senate
b. By a two-thirds vote in the House and a majority in the Senate
c. By a majority vote in both the House and the Senate
d. By a two-thirds vote in both the House and the Senate

76. Who established the precedent for the two-term limit for the US presidency?

a. Abraham Lincoln
b. Alexander Hamilton
c. George Washington
d. Thomas Jefferson

77. What would be considered an informal qualification for being elected President?

a. The President must be well-traveled
b. The President must be at least 40 years old
c. The President must have good character
d. The President must be a natural citizen

78. What was Franklin D. Roosevelt's "court packing" plan?

a. A plan to influence court outcomes by packing the observation gallery with his own supporters.
b. A plan to prevent cases from coming to trial by filing a large number of other cases in order to create judicial gridlock.
c. A plan to keep Roosevelt surrounded by his own supporters to give him a greater impression of popularity.
d. A plan to appoint a second justice for every federal justice over the age of seventy.

79. The concept of due process in the Fifth Amendment to the U.S. Constitution protects individuals in which of the following ways?

  a. Guaranteeing a citizen's right to a trial by jury within a reasonable timeframe
  b. Restricting the government's ability to remove basic rights without following the law
  c. Guaranteeing a citizen's right to equal protection under the law
  d. Restricting the government's ability to remove basic rights without dire cause

80. The Sugar Act (1764), the Stamp Act (1765), and the Townshend Acts (1767-1770) all aroused the American colonists' concerns about:

  a. separation of powers.
  b. taxation without representation.
  c. the right to an impartial and speedy trial.
  d. freedom of speech.

FCLE Practice Test #2

Answer Key and Explanations for Test #2

1. A: The president of the United States serves as commander-in-chief, but the writers of the Constitution, who feared how authority was used by monarchs, limited the president's power in this role. The president cannot declare war or oversee military regulations, although presidents have traditionally authorized the use of force without war being declared.

2. C: The proposal states that public welfare overrides private rights. Choice A is incorrect. The reason is that the proposal does not suggest that Ohio will lose rights to the control of the lake. Choice B is also incorrect. The property owners are said to have a protected right to their land and to be able to give or sell those rights. Choice D is wrong. The reason is that the amendment clearly refers to the lawmakers' response to passing the Great Lakes Water Compact.

3. D: America is a common law country because English common law was adopted in all states except Louisiana. Common law is based on precedent and changes over time. Each state develops its own common laws.

4. A: After a series of disagreements over Reconstruction Policy, Congress passed the Tenure of Office Act, according to which the President needed congressional consent to dismiss from office anyone who had been confirmed by the Senate. President Johnson violated the Act by dismissing Secretary of War Edwin Stanton, whom radical Republicans wanted to keep in office. Congress accordingly impeached President Johnson. Regarding option B, Southern states did enact "Black Laws" to prevent African Americans from voting, but President Johnson was not impeached because he allowed such laws (and thus failed to enforce the Fourteenth Amendment). Johnson did seek to disenfranchise former Confederate officers, and he did attempt to form a third political party; but neither of these actions were grounds for his impeachment (with respect to the former action, radical Republicans were in agreement). This eliminates choices C and D respectively.

5. B: Only the federal government has the power to give copyrights and patents to individuals or companies. The power to levy taxes, borrow money, and spend money (A) is a power shared by federal and state governments. The power to set the criteria that qualify individuals to vote (C) is a power given to state governments only. The power to ratify amendments proposed to the Constitution (D) is a power of only the state governments.

6. B: Shared, or concurrent, powers are those powers held by both the states and the federal government. While the Constitution specifically grants Congress the exclusive power to coin money, it does not specifically forbid the states from building roads, collecting taxes, and establishing courts.

7. D: The Federalist Papers were a series of essays written by Alexander Hamilton, James Madison, and John Jay to bolster support for the ratification of the US Constitution (1787). Federalist No 51, drafted by James Madison in 1788, deals with the division of power within the federal government. In the essay, Madison (a Federalist) addresses concerns presented by the Anti-Federalists (a group of individuals who opposed the ratification of the Constitution) that the proposed system of government places too much power in the hands of the federal government. The Anti-Federalists feared that this concentration would lead to abuses of power and perhaps the development of tyrannical rulers. In Federalist No 51, Madison argues that the Constitution would establish a government in which specific powers are enumerated to each of the three branches of government. As indicated in the excerpt above, Madison also discusses the role of checks and balances in safeguarding against the development of tyranny. Madison, and the Federalists in general, believed

that by incorporating checks and balances into the Constitution, each branch of government would have the ability to limit the power of another branch. For example, the President of the United States has the power to veto legislation passed by Congress. In turn, Congress, with a two-thirds majority vote, can override that presidential veto. The text above is most directly referencing checks and balances, not simply the separation of powers between the three branches (C).

8. B: The Sherman Anti-Trust Act of 1890 was enacted in response to the growth of large monopolies in the period following the end of the Civil War. While its purpose was to prevent restraints on free trade, it was not strictly enforced. Additionally, the wording was vague enough that it was also used to break up labor unions. It was replaced by the Clayton Antitrust Act in 1914.

9. C: Brutus I was the first in a series of essays known as the Anti-Federalist Papers. The Anti-Federalist Papers were designed to counter the claims presented in the Federalist Papers in order to discourage the passage of the US Constitution (1787). Brutus I was published by an anonymous author, believed to be Robert Yates (1738–1801), and reviewed the primary fears of the Anti-Federalists regarding the Constitution and resulting system of government. The essay argued that the Constitution paved the way for a significant concentration of power within the federal government. Brutus warned that this would lead to tyranny and the violation of individual liberties, and he argued that the lack of a bill of rights was especially problematic in light of such strong central authority. Although the Constitution was ultimately ratified, Brutus I raised awareness and concerns regarding the absence of a bill of rights. The Federalists argued that a bill of rights was not necessary, as the government possessed only the rights that were dictated by the Constitution; however, they ultimately agreed to add such protections in exchange for the ratification of the document as a whole. The Bill of Rights was ratified in 1791 and provided for the protection of a variety of essential civil liberties for the people of the United States.

10. D: After the American Revolution, the framers of the American government were concerned that a strong central government could lead to abuses of power. Accordingly, The Articles of Confederation did not grant the federal government the ability to raise taxes. Another restriction was the inability to regulate interstate commerce. Options A, B, and C can all be eliminated because, though the federal government was generally weak under the Articles of Confederation, the Articles granted the federal government each of the powers given in those options.

11. D: In the Dred Scott decision of 1857, the Court ruled that no slave or descendant of slaves could ever be a United States citizen. It also declared the Missouri Compromise of 1820 to be unconstitutional, clearing the way for the expansion of slavery in new American territories. This ruling pleased Southerners and outraged the North, further dividing the nation and setting the stage for war.

12. A: The attitudes of American colonists after the 1763 Treaty of Paris ended the French and Indian War was not a direct contributor to the American Revolution. American colonists had a supportive attitude toward Great Britain then, and were proud of the part they played in winning the war. Their good will was not returned by British leaders, who looked down on American colonials and sought to increase their imperial power over them. Even in 1761, a sign of Americans' objections to having their liberty curtailed by the British was seen when Boston attorney James Otis argued in court against the Writs of Assistance, search warrants to enforce England's mercantilist trade restrictions, as violating the kinds of natural laws espoused during the Enlightenment. Lord George Grenville's aggressive program to defend the North American frontier in the wake of Chief Pontiac's attacks included stricter enforcement of the Navigation Acts, the Proclamation of 1763, the Sugar Act (or Revenue Act), the Currency Act, and most of all the Stamp Act. Colonists objected to these as taxation without representation. Other events followed in this taxation dispute, which

121

Answer Key and Explanations for Test #2

further eroded Americans' relationship with British government, including the Townshend Acts, the Massachusetts Circular Letter, the Boston Massacre, the Tea Act, and the resulting Boston Tea Party. Finally, with Britain's passage of the Intolerable Acts and the Americans' First Continental Congress, which was followed by Britain's military aggression against American resistance, actual warfare began in 1775. While not all of the colonies wanted war or independence by then, things changed by 1776, and Jefferson's Declaration of Independence was formalized. James Otis, Samuel Adams, Patrick Henry, the Sons of Liberty, and the Stamp Act Congress also contributed to the beginning of the American Revolution.

13. D: Federal, state, and local governments use laws, regulations, decisions, and actions to address public issues such as healthcare and determine public policy. Members of the private sector, religious leaders, and institutions influence public policy, but the decision lies with the government.

14. C: Thomas Jefferson embraced John Locke's concept of separation of church and state. Deism posits that a Supernatural force created the world and universe, but that He did not intervene after creation. Jefferson wanted minimal central governing, just as he viewed the Creator's relationship with the universe.

15. C: The people who were opposed to the idea of having a bill of rights in the Constitution were primarily concerned that by specifically enumerating a set of rights, that there would be an argument that the rights not listed did not exist or were not important. The Bill of Rights did not initially apply to the states even though there was some concern that the states were more likely to infringe upon individual liberties than the federal government.

16. A: The president has the authority to negotiate and sign treaties. A two-thirds vote of the Senate, however, is needed to ratify a treaty for it to be upheld.

17. C: The 26th Amendment states: "The right of citizens of the United States, who are 18 years of age or older, to vote, shall not be denied or abridged by the United States or any state on account of age." The 24th Amendment invalidates poll taxes as a requirement to vote. The 25th Amendment deals with presidential succession. The 27th Amendment deals with Congress members' compensation.

18. D: Although the Thirteenth, Fourteenth, and Fifteenth Amendments guaranteed certain legal protection to African Americans, Southern whites were able to retain power by enacting various restrictions on voting. Lacking formal education and deprived of their right to vote, freed slaves were unable to attain political or economic power in the South.

19. B: In the years shown in the chart (1964–1966), the percentage of African Americans in E-6 ranks (Staff Sergeant or Petty Officer, First Class) ranks in the Army, Navy, and Marines all grew. In 1964, African Americans made up 13.9% of the E-6 ranked members of the Army, 4.7% of the E-6 ranked members of the Navy, and 5.0% of the E-6 ranked members of the Marine Corps. By 1966, these numbers were 18.1%, 5.6%, and 10.4%, respectively.

20. B: President John Adams appointed William Marbury as Justice of the Peace, but Secretary of State James Madison never delivered the commission. Marbury claimed that under the Judiciary Act of 1789, the Supreme Court could order his commission be given to him. The Supreme Court denied Marbury's petition citing that the Judiciary Act of 1789 was unconstitutional, although they believed he was entitled to his commission.

21. D: According to Article III of the Constitution, Justices of the Supreme Court, judges of the courts of appeals and district courts, and judges of the Court of International Trade are appointed by the president with the confirmation of the Senate. The judicial branch of the government is the only one not elected by the people.

22. D: The Treaty of Paris of 1783 did state that Britain and the other leading European countries now recognized the United States of America as an independent country. This treaty also set boundaries, but the southern tip of Florida was not the southern boundary (A). It was the northern boundary of Florida, which became a Spanish territory. Therefore, it is not true that Britain kept both Canada and Florida under this treaty (B). Canada did remain a British territory under its terms, but Britain had to cede Florida to Spain. The Treaty of Paris also gave private British creditors freedom to collect debts from Americans, not the reverse (C). The treaty also stipulated that property confiscated from loyalists during the war should be given back, not kept. Other terms of the Treaty of Paris included that the western boundary of the United States would be the Mississippi River.

23. D: The ideal present in the Declaration of Independence (1776) that has been most influential to equal rights movements is the argument that all men are created equal and possess certain unalienable rights. Established by Thomas Jefferson (1743–1826) in 1776 with the drafting of the Declaration of Independence, the belief that all men have the right to basic rights such as the protection of life, liberty, and property served as a foundational principle of the United States government. Initially, this protection extended only to white men who owned property. Later, groups such as abolitionists called on this principle to argue that slavery was an infringement on the natural rights of African Americans. Furthermore, activists working towards women's suffrage also invoked this aspect of the Declaration of Independence, arguing that women's inability to vote positioned them as lesser citizens. Consequently, as time progressed, the principle of equality served as a key foundation for the expansion of civil liberties to all US citizens.

24. B: Despite the constitutional guarantee of free speech, it is not absolute. There are certain restrictions in which laws regulate defamation, slander, libel, conspiracy, and occasions when speech has the potential of causing "imminent harm." During the Vietnam War era, draftees would publicize their displeasure by burning their draft cards—this action actually constituted a federal crime. School employees are required to be socially responsible and are liable to discipline if their actions encourage delinquency or profanity. The laws prohibit threats against the President only when it represents a real threat, not "political hyperbole."

25. C: Line 3 best lists the kinds of cases over which the US federal court system has jurisdiction. The US federal court system has jurisdiction over cases involving constitutional law, bankruptcy, and disputes between states (the federal court system also has jurisdiction over cases concerning US treaties and laws, among other types of cases). State courts have jurisdiction over most contract cases, most criminal cases, and most personal injury cases; this eliminates Line 1, Line 2, and Line 4, each of which list one of those kinds of cases as under the jurisdiction of the US federal court system.

26. C: Alexander Hamilton was the Founding Father who is credited with founding the Federalist Party. Hamilton was a proponent of the idea that the young country required the support of the rich and powerful in order to survive. This party grew out of Hamilton's political connections in Washington and was particularly popular in the northeastern United States. John Adams was a member of this party. George Washington's personal beliefs were most closely aligned with the Federalist Party, but he disliked political parties and refused to become a member of one.

Thomas Jefferson was the founder of the Democratic-Republican Party.

Answer Key and Explanations for Test #2

123

27. A: It is not true that the founding fathers specifically stated in the Constitution that the United States would be a democracy. The founding fathers wanted the new United States to be founded on principles of liberty and equality, but they did not specifically describe these principles with the term *democracy*. Thus, the Declaration of Independence, like the Constitution after it, did not stipulate a democracy, although both did state the principles of equality and freedom. The Constitution also provided for the election of the new government, and for protection of the rights of some, but not all, of the people. Notable exceptions at the time were black people and women. Only later were laws passed to protect their rights over the years.

28. D: In *Guinn v. United States,* the Supreme Court struck down a grandfather clause exempting white voters from a literacy test required of black voters in 1915 (A). Oklahoma then passed a voter registration law in 1916 requiring citizens who had not voted in 1914 to register to vote in 11 days or lose their voting rights. In *Lane v. Wilson,* the Supreme Court invalidated this law in 1939 (B). In *Sipuel v. Board of Regents of University of Oklahoma,* the Supreme Court required Oklahoma to admit a black woman into law school in 1948 (C). After two Supreme Court sessions, with Thurgood Marshall's leadership, the state gave Sipuel a one-person "law school" with two professors, using the State Capitol library. Sipuel returned to state court, arguing this separate-but-equal treatment did not meet Supreme Court standards, still applying to the law school. Eventually, the university president ordered her admission, but she and other black students were segregated. While Sipuel was still there, *McLaurin v. Oklahoma State Regents* remedied this in 1950 (D): The Court ruled segregation removed a graduate student's rights to equal protection under the law, setting precedent for Brown *v. Board of Education* with public schools in 1954.

29. D: Democratic consensus is the term for the general agreement of the people on fundamental principles of governance and the values supporting them.

30. C: The 26th Amendment is the youth voting rights amendment allowing 18-year-olds to vote, signed by President Nixon. The Vietnam War gave more urgency to the "old enough to fight, old enough to vote" slogan. The other amendment choices are in similar time frames and close enough to the 26th Amendment to possibly confuse a student who has not fully studied some of the more important amendments such as the 26th.

31. B: Published in early 1776, *Common Sense* condemned hereditary kingship. The pamphlet was popular in Colonial America, and even George Washington noticed its effect on the general population. Later that same year, Jefferson drafted the Declaration of Independence.

32. D: Because of its isolation at the geographic extremes of the confederacy, Texas slaves were not affected by the 1863 Emancipation Proclamation. After the fall of the confederacy Union troops occupied each of the former Confederate States. Union General Gordon Granger arrived at Galveston with 2000 federal troops on June 19, 1865 and read aloud "General order No. 3" announcing the emancipation of slaves. Each year Juneteenth is celebrated as a holiday in Texas and other states.

33. C: Nebraska does not require voter registration, but all other states do and have their own process. State and local officials administer federal elections, and though each state has its own method for holding elections, federal elections are always held at the same time.

34. D: The Convention, organized by Lucretia Mott and Elizabeth Cady Stanton and held in upstate New York, approved a Declaration of Sentiments that proclaimed the equality of men and women. The first antislavery society in America was founded in Philadelphia in 1775. The Republican Party had its first official meeting in Jackson, Michigan in 1854. The American Temperance Society was established in Boston in 1826.

35. C: The Civil Rights Act of 1964 affected the Jim Crow laws in the Southern states. Many minorities suffered under unfair voting laws and segregation. President Lyndon Johnson signed the Civil Rights Act of 1964 into law after the 1963 assassination of President Kennedy, who championed the reform.

36. D: The Articles of Confederation did formally establish the name of the United States of America (A) for the new confederation. They did allocate just one vote to each state in the Congress of the Confederation (B), to which each state could send two to seven delegates. They did state that the individual states would keep their sovereignty, freedom, and equality (C) with the government of the confederation, and would maintain "...every power, jurisdiction, and right, which is not by this Confederation expressly delegated." The Articles of Confederation were in favor of state militias, but stated that no individual state could form armies or navies, or engage in war, without the permission of Congress.

37. C: Intrastate trade is solely within a state, so the state has jurisdiction over it. Taxation is a right granted to both federal and state authorities. Declaring war is a national decision. Patents and copyrights apply to goods made and/or sold throughout the country; therefore, they are a federal responsibility.

38. B: Plessy v. Ferguson (1896) found that segregated facilities for blacks and whites are not in violation of the Constitution. The doctrine of "separate but equal" was overturned in Brown v. Board of Education (1954). Marbury v. Madison (1803) established the Supreme Court's power to strike down acts of Congress that conflict with the Constitution. Gideon v. Wainwright (1963) guaranteed an attorney to anyone charged with a serious criminal offense.

39. C: The main subject matter of civic responsibility is a person's responsibilities as a citizen. By contrast, the main subject matter of personal responsibility is one's responsibilities as a person. For example, keeping a promise to a friend is often a matter of personal responsibility because such a duty arises from the friendship. Serving on a jury when called to do so is an example of civic responsibility because such a duty arises from the person's citizenship. None of the other options given accurately describe the main subject matter of civic responsibility. For example, while a journalist might see accurate reporting of government actions as his or her civic responsibility, such reporting is not the main subject matter of civic responsibility and is also a responsibility that arises from that journalist's employment. Similar reasoning applies to a person's responsibilities as a government worker. This eliminates options A and D. Civic responsibility does not primarily concern inter-government relations; this eliminates option B.

40. B: *Marbury v. Madison* started with the election of Thomas Jefferson as third President of the United States. The lame-duck Congress responded by issuing a large number of judicial patents, which the incoming president and Secretary of State refused to deliver to their holders. Marbury, who was to receive a patent as Justice of the Peace, sued to demand delivery. What makes this case important is the decision which declared the judiciary's ability to overturn legislation that conflicted with the Constitution. The case states:

"It is emphatically the province and duty of the judicial department to say what the law is. Those who apply the rule to particular cases must, of necessity, expound and interpret that rule. If two laws conflict with each other, the courts must decide on the operation of each.

"So if a law be in opposition to the Constitution; if both the law and the constitution apply to a particular case, so that the court must either decide that case conformably to the law, disregarding the Constitution; or conformably to the Constitution, disregarding the law; the court must determine which of these conflicting rules governs the case. This is of the very essence of judicial duty.

"If, then, the courts are to regard the Constitution, and the Constitution is superior to any ordinary act of the legislature, the Constitution, and not such ordinary act, must govern the case to which they both apply."

Later, the ruling states: "The judicial power of the United States is extended to all cases arising under the Constitution." It was in this way that the Supreme Court achieved its now traditional ability to strike down laws and to act as the final arbitrator of what is and is not allowed under the US Constitution.

41. A: The word "democracy" comes from two Greek root words: *demos* "people" and *kratia* "rule."

42. C: The correct answer is C. Constitutional republics provide individual rights in their Constitutions. The people elect representatives, and representatives' policies are moderated by constitutional guidelines.

43. A: The Supreme Court decision in *Gibbons v. Ogden* ruled that Congress has the power to regulate interstate commerce via the Constitution's Commerce Clause. The decision in *Ableman v. Booth* (B) ruled that State courts cannot rule to contradict Federal court rulings. The decision in *Plessy v. Ferguson* (C) ruled that "separate but equal" segregation was constitutional. The decision in The *Paquete Habana* (D) ruled that customary international law could be used as a reference by Federal courts because it is integrated as part of American law. Except for choice A, none of these other decisions specifically involved regulating interstate navigation.

44. A: The 10th Amendment establishes that any power not given to the federal government in the Constitution belongs to the states or the people. The federal and local governments share many responsibilities.

45. A: The Magna Carta was a document signed in 1215 by King John of England that was written to limit the power of the King of England. The document established important principles such as the rule of law and due process, influencing many of the future foundational documents of US democracy. The text above is from the Due Process Clause of the Fifth Amendment, which declares that the essential freedoms of life, liberty, and property cannot be taken away without due process, or fair legal proceedings. The principle of due process was established in the Magna Carta, as it stated no man should be exiled or lose his rights without lawful judgment by a jury of his peers. This prevented the British monarchy from engaging in unfair treatment of the accused and promoted equitable legal proceedings.

46. B: Thomas Jefferson (1743–1826) is credited as the primary author of the Declaration of Independence. In 1776, in response to injustices committed by the British Monarchy, the Continental Congress established a five-man committee to draft the Declaration of Independence, with Jefferson selected as the main author because of his eloquent writing style and position as a prominent politician from Virginia. When drafting the document, Jefferson relied heavily on Enlightenment ideals, especially those of political philosopher John Locke (1632–1704). Under Jefferson's leadership, the Declaration of Independence outlined the colonists' desire to gain independence as well as the importance of protecting certain inalienable rights. Ultimately, Jefferson's work was revised by the established committee and voted on by the Continental

Congress prior to its adoption on July 4, 1776. The other answer choices are also important foundational documents drafted by prominent political thinkers of the time; Federalist No 10 (1787) (A) was authored by James Madison, the US Constitution (1787) (C) was penned primarily by James Madison with assistance by Alexander Hamilton and John Jay, and the Articles of Confederation (1777) (D) is generally credited to John Dickinson.

47. B: The Senate Committee on Homeland Security and Government Affairs is a standing committee that oversees and reforms government operations and exercises the congressional power of government oversight.

48. B: The President may veto legislation passed by Congress. The executive branch has this "check" on the legislative branch.

49. B: Most presidents have only served two terms, a precedent established by George Washington. Ulysses S. Grant and Theodore Roosevelt sought third terms; however, only Franklin D. Roosevelt served more than two terms. He served a third term and won a fourth, but died in its first year. The 22nd Amendment was passed by Congress in 1947 and ratified in 1951. It officially limited the president to two terms, and a vice president who serves two years as president only can be elected for one term.

50. A: Choice D sounds like a good option, because this is something that did happen, but it happened before the Dawes Act. The Nez Perce conflict of 1877 also occurred before the Dawes Act, so choice C is incorrect. Choice B was the hope of Dawes and other American politicians who planned the act in order to try to help "assimilate" Native Americans, but that was not the practical result as much as choice A, the taking over of reservation lands away from Native Americans.

51. C: A federalist system of government is a government under which power is shared by a central authority and sub-components of the federation. In the United States in particular, power is shared by the federal government and the individual states. Option A, that the legislative branch consists of two representative bodies (the House of Representatives and the Senate) is true, of course, but does not describe a uniquely federalist structure. Rather, it describes the concept of bicameralism. Option A may thus be eliminated. Option B, likewise, describes different types of democracy but not federalism. Option B can thus be eliminated. Regarding option D, this statement is also true (the US Constitution shapes national legislation) but it is not a descriptive statement of the federalist system because the statement makes no mention that power is shared by the states.

52. C: It is the BEST and only definition of the initiative process: It allowed citizens to introduce legislation proposals at a local or state level by gathering petitions, and proposals would then be addressed by lawmakers or placed on ballots for a vote. The other answer choices give definitions of "referendum" (choice A), "recall" (choice B), and also describe simply visiting a state legislature to give testimony about an issue (choice D), none of which define the "initiative" process.

53. D: Both answer A and answer C furthered the civil rights cause, but answer B impeded this cause. In the case of *Brown v. Board of Education of Topeka*, the Supreme Court's 1954 ruling stated that schools segregated by race are by nature not equal. This ruling was monumental in the NAACP's fight against school segregation. Orval Faubus, Governor of Arkansas, tried to prevent Little Rock High School's integration in 1957 (B). The situation escalated to the point that President Eisenhower nationalized the Arkansas National Guard and sent the 101st Airborne Division to protect the high school students from harm (C). These actions furthered civil rights by showing the government's defense of school integration.

54. C: Prior to the Seventeenth Amendment, adopted in 1913, US senators were chosen by state legislatures rather than by popular state elections. The former system caused problems beginning in the mid-nineteenth century, problems exacerbated by the fact that there was no consistent process among the states for just how state legislatures chose their US Senators. The Seventeenth Amendment required that US Senators be chosen by direct popular election by the citizens of the relevant state. The Seventeenth Amendment did not concern state senators (i.e., senators serving state Senates), governors, or censuses to determine the appropriate level of representation in a House of Representatives. This eliminates options A, B, and D.

55. C: Mother Jones wanted laws to protect child workers. Legislators finally responded to appeals from her and others. None of the other answer choices would logically follow. The words would not have been an encouragement for children to work in factories. So, choice A is incorrect. Choice B is also not right. The South continued to be a major textile region. Increasing pay for child labor was not the solution to the problem. So, choice D is incorrect.

56. A: Federalist No 31, written by Alexander Hamilton, reiterated the need for a strong federal government. Hamilton argued that the power that would be granted to the federal government by the US Constitution would allow the government to effectively manage national concerns, especially in the areas of defense and taxation. Furthermore, Hamilton asserted that the ability of the federal government to levy taxes was necessary to raise the revenue needed to maintain order and manage the daily operations of the US government. In accordance with Hamilton's views and based on the failures of the Articles of Confederation (the first governing doctrine of the United States), the ability to levy taxes was necessary to manage an effective government and union. Article I, Section 8, Clause 1 of the US Constitution (1787) describes the power of the United States Congress to "lay and collect taxes" so that national debts can be paid and the general welfare and military provided for.

57. D: Congress did not have the authority to levy taxes under the Articles of Confederation. Without the ability to levy taxes, there was no way to finance programs, which weakened the government.

58. B: The Mayflower Compact was signed in 1620 by the Pilgrims aboard the Mayflower. By signing the document, the Pilgrims created a social contract in which they agreed to establish a system of government that operated based on the collective good of the colony. Social contract theory, or the notion that political power is derived from consent of the governed and that those individuals agree to follow predetermined rules in exchange for protection, is an important tenet of early American society as well as modern American government. While the Mayflower Compact did not establish a fully democratic society, it set an important precedent of self-governance and governmental authority based on the consent and will of the citizenry.

59. B: Judges who are eligible to retire but still work are called senior judges. Retired judges who occasionally hear cases are called recalled judges. Both senior and recalled judges handle about 15-20 percent of district and appellate court caseloads.

60. B: A strict constructionist, Jefferson argued that that the Constitution did not make any provision for the creation of a federal bank. Jefferson was a leader of the Democratic-Republicans who opposed the establishment of a powerful central government. He believed that the Bank would give an unfair advantage to the more industrial northern states.

61. A: America has a history of organized political protest dating back to the American Revolution. The right to peaceful protest is protected by the First Amendment. The American labor union movement, the antislavery movement, the women's suffrage movement, and the civil rights movement all used political protest to gain support for their causes.

62. C: *Common Sense*, a pamphlet written by Thomas Paine (1737–1809) in 1775, served as an important foundation for the decision of the American colonists to declare independence from England. Paine argued that the concentration of power in the hands of one individual on the basis of heredity was unnatural and resulted in unjust treatment of a monarch's subjects. Furthermore, Paine reprimanded King George III (1738–1820) for his tyrannical tendencies and blatant abuses of power. The critique directly influenced the Declaration of Independence in its list of grievances against King George III, an exhaustive list which highlighted the concerns of the colonists and their justifications for their formal declaration of independence. These points underscored the argument presented by Paine questioning the logic in maintaining America's position as a colonial state under a distant monarch. Ultimately, the pamphlet laid the groundwork for a government that operated only with the consent of the governed.

63. A: Representative government, by which citizens elect officials who share their views and who, in turn, present their views in a democratic system, is not a true democracy in which each individual votes on each issue. As the population of a democracy grows, the practicality of every individual voting on every issue becomes prohibitive to the process.

64. A: A bill is a proposed law.

65. D: The vice president also serves as the president of the Senate. If a tie occurs in the Senate, the vice president casts his vote to break the tie.

66. D: The Office of Management and Budget is part of the Executive Office of the President (EOP). The EOP is a group of Presidential advisers and has been in place since Theodore Roosevelt. The President appoints members directly, but some positions like the Director of the Office of Management and Budget need Senate approval.

67. A: If there is a tie in the Electoral College, each state's delegation in the House of Representatives gets a vote, and the majority wins. The Senate votes on the Vice President who becomes acting President if the House does not come to a conclusion by Inauguration Day. It is possible for the Senate to tie because the former Vice President is not allowed to vote.

68. C: The speech is from President Richard M. Nixon, who was about to become, in 1972, the first US president to visit the People's Republic of China. The other presidents listed are good guesses as they are from similar time periods and might have made similar speeches about China and the Soviet Union, but they are incorrect choices.

69. C: Colonists did find that tea shipped directly by the British East India Company cost less than smuggled Dutch tea, even with tax. The colonists, however, did not buy it. They refused, despite its lower cost, on the principle that the British were taxing colonists without representation. It is true that the British East India Company lost money as a result of colonists buying tea smuggled from Holland. They sought to remedy this problem by getting concessions from Parliament to ship tea directly to the colonies instead of going through England as the Navigation Acts normally required. Boston Governor Thomas Hutchinson, who sided with Britain, stopped tea ships from leaving the harbor, which after 20 days would cause the tea to be sold at auction. At that time, British taxes on the tea would be paid. On the 19th night after Hutchinson's action, American protestors held the Boston Tea Party, dressing as Native Americans and dumping all the tea into the harbor to destroy it so it could not be taxed and sold. Many American colonists disagreed with the Boston Tea Party because it involved destroying private property. When Lord North and the British Parliament responded by passing the Coercive Acts and the Quebec Act, known collectively in America as the Intolerable Acts, Americans changed their minds, siding with the Bostonians against the British.

70. A: Article II of the Constitution gives the House of Representatives the sole power of impeachment and the Senate the sole power to convict. The Chief Justice of the United States is empowered to preside over the Senate trial of a President.

71. C: The Federalist Papers were written and published anonymously by John Jay, Alexander Hamilton, and James Madison as part of their effort to ratify the Constitution. There are 85 letters in total and they were meant to convince normal Americans that they should support the Constitution by explaining what it meant and what it was intended to accomplish.

72. A: The concept of mixed government dates back to antiquity. Plato and Aristotle both advocated a mixture of monarchic, aristocratic, oligarchic, and democratic governments to prevent a single class, state, or person from taking absolute power. The separation of powers in government preserves the principle of mixed government.

73. C: In a unitary system of government, almost all control is held by the central government. The central government makes the laws, and the local governments are not allowed to overrule them. Although the unitary system is often associated with repressive regimes like that of North Korea, it also exists in countries like Japan and Great Britain. A unitary system tends to work better in countries with homogenous populations and relatively little cultural difference between regions. A federation, meanwhile, is a system in which the central government has some powers but grants others to local governments. The United States is a federation. A democracy is a system in which the people elect government officials. A democracy could be a unitary system, but it does not have to be. In a confederation, the central government has much less power than the regional and local governments. In such a system, the central government is usually only responsible for defense and trade with other nations.

74. C: The Constitution was not ratified immediately. Only five states accepted it in early 1788; Massachusetts, New York, Rhode Island, and Virginia were originally opposed to the Constitution. Rhode Island reluctantly accepted it in 1790.

75. D: The process of overriding a presidential veto is described in Article I, Section 7 of the Constitution. It requires a two-thirds vote from both the House and the Senate.

76. C: George Washington served 2 four-year terms as president. This interval of time was not specified in the Constitution, but future presidents followed suit (until FDR).

77. C: Informal qualifications are the public's expectations of Presidential candidates. These can vary, but the President is considered by many to be a moral leader. This means the public expects the President to have a strong character, so a criminal record or lapses in moral judgment can prevent a person from becoming President.

78. D: The New Deal met with conservative opposition, especially in the Supreme Court, whose conservative justices frequently blocked New Deal legislation. The plan that was dubbed the "court packing" plan was to appoint a second justice for every justice over the age of seventy. Because all of the conservative justices on the Supreme Court were over seventy, this would have given Roosevelt the ability to appoint enough justices to swing the Court to his favor. However, this plan was met with extreme popular disapproval which led to its eventual abandonment.

79. B: Under the Fifth Amendment to the U.S. Constitution, the government may not strip certain basic rights from citizens without following the law. In the language of the Fifth Amendment itself, a person shall not "be deprived of life, liberty, or property without due process of law." Of all the options, option B is the only one that accurately describes the concept of due process as understood in the Fifth Amendment. Because due process does not explicitly guarantee a trial by jury within a reasonable timeframe, nor equal protection under the law (concepts covered elsewhere in the Constitution), options A and C can be rejected. Option D can be rejected because the Constitution restricts the government's ability to take away certain rights without following the law, not without a "dire cause" (such as the threat of imminent attack).

80. B: All of these acts of Parliament were intended to raise revenue at the expense of the colonies. The colonists challenged Parliament's right to levy tax on them without their express consent.

Answer Key and Explanations for Test #2

How to Overcome Test Anxiety

Just the thought of taking a test is enough to make most people a little nervous. A test is an important event that can have a long-term impact on your future, so it's important to take it seriously and it's natural to feel anxious about performing well. But just because anxiety is normal, that doesn't mean that it's helpful in test taking, or that you should simply accept it as part of your life. Anxiety can have a variety of effects. These effects can be mild, like making you feel slightly nervous, or severe, like blocking your ability to focus or remember even a simple detail.

If you experience test anxiety—whether severe or mild—it's important to know how to beat it. To discover this, first you need to understand what causes test anxiety.

Causes of Test Anxiety

While we often think of anxiety as an uncontrollable emotional state, it can actually be caused by simple, practical things. One of the most common causes of test anxiety is that a person does not feel adequately prepared for their test. This feeling can be the result of many different issues such as poor study habits or lack of organization, but the most common culprit is time management. Starting to study too late, failing to organize your study time to cover all of the material, or being distracted while you study will mean that you're not well prepared for the test. This may lead to cramming the night before, which will cause you to be physically and mentally exhausted for the test. Poor time management also contributes to feelings of stress, fear, and hopelessness as you realize you are not well prepared but don't know what to do about it.

Other times, test anxiety is not related to your preparation for the test but comes from unresolved fear. This may be a past failure on a test, or poor performance on tests in general. It may come from comparing yourself to others who seem to be performing better or from the stress of living up to expectations. Anxiety may be driven by fears of the future—how failure on this test would affect your educational and career goals. These fears are often completely irrational, but they can still negatively impact your test performance.

Elements of Test Anxiety

As mentioned earlier, test anxiety is considered to be an emotional state, but it has physical and mental components as well. Sometimes you may not even realize that you are suffering from test anxiety until you notice the physical symptoms. These can include trembling hands, rapid heartbeat, sweating, nausea, and tense muscles. Extreme anxiety may lead to fainting or vomiting. Obviously, any of these symptoms can have a negative impact on testing. It is important to recognize them as soon as they begin to occur so that you can address the problem before it damages your performance.

The mental components of test anxiety include trouble focusing and inability to remember learned information. During a test, your mind is on high alert, which can help you recall information and stay focused for an extended period of time. However, anxiety interferes with your mind's natural processes, causing you to blank out, even on the questions you know well. The strain of testing during anxiety makes it difficult to stay focused, especially on a test that may take several hours. Extreme anxiety can take a huge mental toll, making it difficult not only to recall test information but even to understand the test questions or pull your thoughts together.

Effects of Test Anxiety

Test anxiety is like a disease—if left untreated, it will get progressively worse. Anxiety leads to poor performance, and this reinforces the feelings of fear and failure, which in turn lead to poor performances on subsequent tests. It can grow from a mild nervousness to a crippling condition. If allowed to progress, test anxiety can have a big impact on your schooling, and consequently on your future.

Test anxiety can spread to other parts of your life. Anxiety on tests can become anxiety in any stressful situation, and blanking on a test can turn into panicking in a job situation. But fortunately, you don't have to let anxiety rule your testing and determine your grades. There are a number of relatively simple steps you can take to move past anxiety and function normally on a test and in the rest of life.

Physical Steps for Beating Test Anxiety

While test anxiety is a serious problem, the good news is that it can be overcome. It doesn't have to control your ability to think and remember information. While it may take time, you can begin taking steps today to beat anxiety.

Just as your first hint that you may be struggling with anxiety comes from the physical symptoms, the first step to treating it is also physical. Rest is crucial for having a clear, strong mind. If you are tired, it is much easier to give in to anxiety. But if you establish good sleep habits, your body and mind will be ready to perform optimally, without the strain of exhaustion. Additionally, sleeping well helps you to retain information better, so you're more likely to recall the answers when you see the test questions.

Getting good sleep means more than going to bed on time. It's important to allow your brain time to relax. Take study breaks from time to time so it doesn't get overworked, and don't study right before bed. Take time to rest your mind before trying to rest your body, or you may find it difficult to fall asleep.

Along with sleep, other aspects of physical health are important in preparing for a test. Good nutrition is vital for good brain function. Sugary foods and drinks may give a burst of energy but this burst is followed by a crash, both physically and emotionally. Instead, fuel your body with protein and vitamin-rich foods.

Also, drink plenty of water. Dehydration can lead to headaches and exhaustion, especially if your brain is already under stress from the rigors of the test. Particularly if your test is a long one, drink water during the breaks. And if possible, take an energy-boosting snack to eat between sections.

Along with sleep and diet, a third important part of physical health is exercise. Maintaining a steady workout schedule is helpful, but even taking 5-minute study breaks to walk can help get your blood pumping faster and clear your head. Exercise also releases endorphins, which contribute to a positive feeling and can help combat test anxiety.

When you nurture your physical health, you are also contributing to your mental health. If your body is healthy, your mind is much more likely to be healthy as well. So take time to rest, nourish your body with healthy food and water, and get moving as much as possible. Taking these physical steps will make you stronger and more able to take the mental steps necessary to overcome test anxiety.

How to Overcome Test Anxiety

133

Mental Steps for Beating Test Anxiety

Working on the mental side of test anxiety can be more challenging, but as with the physical side, there are clear steps you can take to overcome it. As mentioned earlier, test anxiety often stems from lack of preparation, so the obvious solution is to prepare for the test. Effective studying may be the most important weapon you have for beating test anxiety, but you can and should employ several other mental tools to combat fear.

First, boost your confidence by reminding yourself of past success—tests or projects that you aced. If you're putting as much effort into preparing for this test as you did for those, there's no reason you should expect to fail here. Work hard to prepare; then trust your preparation.

Second, surround yourself with encouraging people. It can be helpful to find a study group, but be sure that the people you're around will encourage a positive attitude. If you spend time with others who are anxious or cynical, this will only contribute to your own anxiety. Look for others who are motivated to study hard from a desire to succeed, not from a fear of failure.

Third, reward yourself. A test is physically and mentally tiring, even without anxiety, and it can be helpful to have something to look forward to. Plan an activity following the test, regardless of the outcome, such as going to a movie or getting ice cream.

When you are taking the test, if you find yourself beginning to feel anxious, remind yourself that you know the material. Visualize successfully completing the test. Then take a few deep, relaxing breaths and return to it. Work through the questions carefully but with confidence, knowing that you are capable of succeeding.

Developing a healthy mental approach to test taking will also aid in other areas of life. Test anxiety affects more than just the actual test—it can be damaging to your mental health and even contribute to depression. It's important to beat test anxiety before it becomes a problem for more than testing.

Study Strategy

Being prepared for the test is necessary to combat anxiety, but what does being prepared look like? You may study for hours on end and still not feel prepared. What you need is a strategy for test prep. The next few pages outline our recommended steps to help you plan out and conquer the challenge of preparation.

STEP 1: SCOPE OUT THE TEST

Learn everything you can about the format (multiple choice, essay, etc.) and what will be on the test. Gather any study materials, course outlines, or sample exams that may be available. Not only will this help you to prepare, but knowing what to expect can help to alleviate test anxiety.

STEP 2: MAP OUT THE MATERIAL

Look through the textbook or study guide and make note of how many chapters or sections it has. Then divide these over the time you have. For example, if a book has 15 chapters and you have five days to study, you need to cover three chapters each day. Even better, if you have the time, leave an extra day at the end for overall review after you have gone through the material in depth.

If time is limited, you may need to prioritize the material. Look through it and make note of which sections you think you already have a good grasp on, and which need review. While you are studying, skim quickly through the familiar sections and take more time on the challenging parts.

134

Write out your plan so you don't get lost as you go. Having a written plan also helps you feel more in control of the study, so anxiety is less likely to arise from feeling overwhelmed at the amount to cover.

STEP 3: GATHER YOUR TOOLS

Decide what study method works best for you. Do you prefer to highlight in the book as you study and then go back over the highlighted portions? Or do you type out notes of the important information? Or is it helpful to make flashcards that you can carry with you? Assemble the pens, index cards, highlighters, post-it notes, and any other materials you may need so you won't be distracted by getting up to find things while you study.

If you're having a hard time retaining the information or organizing your notes, experiment with different methods. For example, try color-coding by subject with colored pens, highlighters, or post-it notes. If you learn better by hearing, try recording yourself reading your notes so you can listen while in the car, working out, or simply sitting at your desk. Ask a friend to quiz you from your flashcards, or try teaching someone the material to solidify it in your mind.

STEP 4: CREATE YOUR ENVIRONMENT

It's important to avoid distractions while you study. This includes both the obvious distractions like visitors and the subtle distractions like an uncomfortable chair (or a too-comfortable couch that makes you want to fall asleep). Set up the best study environment possible: good lighting and a comfortable work area. If background music helps you focus, you may want to turn it on, but otherwise keep the room quiet. If you are using a computer to take notes, be sure you don't have any other windows open, especially applications like social media, games, or anything else that could distract you. Silence your phone and turn off notifications. Be sure to keep water close by so you stay hydrated while you study (but avoid unhealthy drinks and snacks).

Also, take into account the best time of day to study. Are you freshest first thing in the morning? Try to set aside some time then to work through the material. Is your mind clearer in the afternoon or evening? Schedule your study session then. Another method is to study at the same time of day that you will take the test, so that your brain gets used to working on the material at that time and will be ready to focus at test time.

STEP 5: STUDY!

Once you have done all the study preparation, it's time to settle into the actual studying. Sit down, take a few moments to settle your mind so you can focus, and begin to follow your study plan. Don't give in to distractions or let yourself procrastinate. This is your time to prepare so you'll be ready to fearlessly approach the test. Make the most of the time and stay focused.

Of course, you don't want to burn out. If you study too long you may find that you're not retaining the information very well. Take regular study breaks. For example, taking five minutes out of every hour to walk briskly, breathing deeply and swinging your arms, can help your mind stay fresh.

As you get to the end of each chapter or section, it's a good idea to do a quick review. Remind yourself of what you learned and work on any difficult parts. When you feel that you've mastered the material, move on to the next part. At the end of your study session, briefly skim through your notes again.

But while review is helpful, cramming last minute is NOT. If at all possible, work ahead so that you won't need to fit all your study into the last day. Cramming overloads your brain with more information than it can process and retain, and your tired mind may struggle to recall even

How to Overcome Test Anxiety

previously learned information when it is overwhelmed with last-minute study. Also, the urgent nature of cramming and the stress placed on your brain contribute to anxiety. You'll be more likely to go to the test feeling unprepared and having trouble thinking clearly.

So don't cram, and don't stay up late before the test, even just to review your notes at a leisurely pace. Your brain needs rest more than it needs to go over the information again. In fact, plan to finish your studies by noon or early afternoon the day before the test. Give your brain the rest of the day to relax or focus on other things, and get a good night's sleep. Then you will be fresh for the test and better able to recall what you've studied.

STEP 6: TAKE A PRACTICE TEST

Many courses offer sample tests, either online or in the study materials. This is an excellent resource to check whether you have mastered the material, as well as to prepare for the test format and environment.

Check the test format ahead of time: the number of questions, the type (multiple choice, free response, etc.), and the time limit. Then create a plan for working through them. For example, if you have 30 minutes to take a 60-question test, your limit is 30 seconds per question. Spend less time on the questions you know well so that you can take more time on the difficult ones.

If you have time to take several practice tests, take the first one open book, with no time limit. Work through the questions at your own pace and make sure you fully understand them. Gradually work up to taking a test under test conditions: sit at a desk with all study materials put away and set a timer. Pace yourself to make sure you finish the test with time to spare and go back to check your answers if you have time.

After each test, check your answers. On the questions you missed, be sure you understand why you missed them. Did you misread the question (tests can use tricky wording)? Did you forget the information? Or was it something you hadn't learned? Go back and study any shaky areas that the practice tests reveal.

Taking these tests not only helps with your grade, but also aids in combating test anxiety. If you're already used to the test conditions, you're less likely to worry about it, and working through tests until you're scoring well gives you a confidence boost. Go through the practice tests until you feel comfortable, and then you can go into the test knowing that you're ready for it.

Test Tips

On test day, you should be confident, knowing that you've prepared well and are ready to answer the questions. But aside from preparation, there are several test day strategies you can employ to maximize your performance.

First, as stated before, get a good night's sleep the night before the test (and for several nights before that, if possible). Go into the test with a fresh, alert mind rather than staying up late to study.

Try not to change too much about your normal routine on the day of the test. It's important to eat a nutritious breakfast, but if you normally don't eat breakfast at all, consider eating just a protein bar. If you're a coffee drinker, go ahead and have your normal coffee. Just make sure you time it so that the caffeine doesn't wear off right in the middle of your test. Avoid sugary beverages, and drink enough water to stay hydrated but not so much that you need a restroom break 10 minutes into the test. If your test isn't first thing in the morning, consider going for a walk or doing a light workout before the test to get your blood flowing.

Allow yourself enough time to get ready, and leave for the test with plenty of time to spare so you won't have the anxiety of scrambling to arrive in time. Another reason to be early is to select a good seat. It's helpful to sit away from doors and windows, which can be distracting. Find a good seat, get out your supplies, and settle your mind before the test begins.

When the test begins, start by going over the instructions carefully, even if you already know what to expect. Make sure you avoid any careless mistakes by following the directions.

Then begin working through the questions, pacing yourself as you've practiced. If you're not sure on an answer, don't spend too much time on it, and don't let it shake your confidence. Either skip it and come back later, or eliminate as many wrong answers as possible and guess among the remaining ones. Don't dwell on these questions as you continue—put them out of your mind and focus on what lies ahead.

Be sure to read all of the answer choices, even if you're sure the first one is the right answer. Sometimes you'll find a better one if you keep reading. But don't second-guess yourself if you do immediately know the answer. Your gut instinct is usually right. Don't let test anxiety rob you of the information you know.

If you have time at the end of the test (and if the test format allows), go back and review your answers. Be cautious about changing any, since your first instinct tends to be correct, but make sure you didn't misread any of the questions or accidentally mark the wrong answer choice. Look over any you skipped and make an educated guess.

At the end, leave the test feeling confident. You've done your best, so don't waste time worrying about your performance or wishing you could change anything. Instead, celebrate the successful completion of this test. And finally, use this test to learn how to deal with anxiety even better next time.

> **Review Video: Test Anxiety**
> Visit mometrix.com/academy and enter code: 100340

Important Qualification

Not all anxiety is created equal. If your test anxiety is causing major issues in your life beyond the classroom or testing center, or if you are experiencing troubling physical symptoms related to your anxiety, it may be a sign of a serious physiological or psychological condition. If this sounds like your situation, we strongly encourage you to seek professional help.

How to Overcome Test Anxiety

Online Resources

Due to our efforts to try to keep this book to a manageable length, we've created a link that will give you access to all of your online resources:

mometrix.com/resources719/fcle

It's Your Moment, Let's Celebrate It!

Share your story @mometrixtestpreparation